Exploring Famous Urban Legends: Uncovering The Truth Behind Mysterious Stories

Pille Pat Du

Published by Pille Pat Du, 2024.

While every precaution has been taken in the preparation of this book, the publisher assumes no responsibility for errors or omissions, or for damages resulting from the use of the information contained herein.

EXPLORING FAMOUS URBAN LEGENDS: UNCOVERING THE TRUTH BEHIND MYSTERIOUS STORIES

First edition. May 17, 2024.

ISBN: 979-8224455201

Written by Pille Pat Du.

Table of Contents

Chapter 1: Introduction

WHAT IS AN URBAN LEGEND?

To understand urban legends, it is essential to recognize their distinct qualities. One of the defining characteristics of an urban legend is their anonymity or lack of a clear origin. Unlike traditional folklore that often has identifiable creators or communities attached to it, urban legends thrive in the realm of uncertainty. They are stories that seemingly originate from nowhere, making it challenging to trace their roots. This lack of attribution often adds to their mystique and contributes to their enduring appeal. Moreover, urban legends typically relate to contemporary societal concerns and anxieties, making them relatable to a wide audience. They often touch on themes such as crime, technology, the supernatural, or unusual events, allowing people to easily connect with the narratives.

Another crucial aspect of urban legends is their mode of transmission. These tales are predominantly spread through oral storytelling, email forwards, social media, or various other forms of communication. The power of storytelling lies in its ability to create a personal connection with the listener, evoking emotions and encouraging active participation. Urban legends thrive on this interpersonal connection, captivating individuals and providing a sense of shared experience.

The subject matter of urban legends is as diverse as the human imagination itself. These tales can revolve around ominous entities like ghosts, monsters, or creatures from mythology, offering people an opportunity to explore the supernatural realm in a controlled environment. They can also center around shocking events, such as gruesome crimes or bizarre occurrences, which both captivate and disturb the audience. Moreover, urban legends often serve as cautionary tales, delivering a moral lesson or warning about the potential dangers of certain behaviors, places, or individuals. They tap into our primal instincts for survival and preservation, reminding us to be vigilant in an unpredictable world.

The allure of urban legends lies in their ability to play on our emotions and spark our imagination. They serve as a form of entertainment, allowing people to experience fear, excitement, or even a sense of wonder in a safe and controlled manner. We share these stories with friends, family, and colleagues, spreading the thrill and intrigue far and wide. The lack of evidence or concrete proof often adds to their longevity. We are left questioning their authenticity, allowing the legends to continue to exist within our collective memory and conversations.

While urban legends hold an undeniable fascination, it is crucial to approach them with a critical mindset. Given their characteristics of anonymity, lack of evidence, and potential for exaggeration, it is essential to scrutinize the information presented within these narratives. Often, urban legends are debunked or proven false, serving as a reminder that not everything we hear is rooted in truth. However, even in their fictional or embellished nature, urban legends can provide valuable insights into contemporary culture, fears, and concerns. By analyzing the underlying themes and societal context, urban legends can serve as a reflection of our collective psyche and the issues that hold our attention. Rooted in the uncertain and lacking clear origins, these tales touch upon our deepest fears, desires, and anxieties. With their diverse subjects and cautionary themes, urban legends provide us with a controlled environment to explore the supernatural, shocking events, and the potential dangers we face. While it is essential to approach urban legends with a critical mindset, the study of these narratives offers valuable insights into our collective imagination and the concerns that resonate within our communities. As we continue to share these stories, urban legends will persist, connecting us through our shared experiences and shared fears.

Why are urban legends so intriguing?

Urban legends have been captivating individuals for generations, captivating listeners in both casual settings and academic circles. These fascinating narratives have sparked curiosity and intrigue, prompting us to marvel at the human inclination to believe in the extraordinary. The allure of urban legends lies in their ability to captivate and entertain while serving as cautionary tales or markers of cultural beliefs and anxieties. Through the examination of various psychological, cultural, and social factors, this book aims to shed light on why urban legends possess such an enduring fascination.

The Psychology Behind Urban Legends

One key aspect of urban legends that renders them so intriguing lies in the psychological mechanisms at play. Our brains have an innate proclivity for storytelling, seeking patterns and narratives to make sense of the world around us. Urban legends tap into this desire, presenting seemingly plausible stories that engage our imagination and evoke a range of emotional responses. From spine-tingling fear to awe-inspiring wonder, urban legends captivate our minds by tapping into our deepest fears, desires, and beliefs. The power of these stories lies in their ability to exploit cognitive biases, shaping our perception of reality and leaving an indelible mark on our collective consciousness.

Cultural Significance of Urban Legends

Urban legends possess an intangible cultural value that further adds to their intrigue. They often serve as social commentaries, reflecting prevalent anxieties, beliefs, and values within a given society or community. These legends become vessels through which societal taboos, fears, and desires are conveyed, allowing individuals to explore and process complex emotions within the safety of a fictional narrative. As cultural artifacts, urban legends act as mirrors that reflect the zeitgeist, capturing the essence of particular time periods and cultural milieus. Through their transmission from person to person, new layers of meaning and interpretation are added, leading urban legends to become symbols of shared experiences and collective memory.

The Role of Social Contagion in Urban Legends

Another aspect contributing to the intrigue surrounding urban legends is their ability to spread rapidly through social networks. This phenomenon, known as social contagion, plays a pivotal role in enhancing their salience and allure. The psychological need to share captivating stories and our inherent desire to belong to communities drives the proliferation of urban legends. Stories that tap into deeply rooted fears or exploit cultural anxieties grab our attention, compelling us to share them with others, thereby ensuring the stories' continuity. Urban legends thrive and evolve within the intricate web of interpersonal connections, providing a sense of cohesion among individuals who share these narratives.

The Evolution of Urban Legends in the Digital Age

While urban legends were once primarily transmitted orally, the advent of the digital age has revolutionized their dissemination. The rise of the internet and social media platforms has transformed the way urban legends are shared, perpetuating their allure and accelerating their diffusion. These digital platforms provide fertile ground for the breeding of new urban legends, remixing and adapting older narratives or giving birth to entirely new ones. The viral nature of online content amplifies the speed and breadth of their dissemination, making urban legends more accessible and appealing to a global audience. The evolution of urban legends in the digital age further underscores their timeless allure and serves as a testament to our insatiable appetite for captivating narratives.

Debunking Urban Legends: Unmasking the Intrigue

Despite their intrigue, urban legends often exist in a gray area, leaving individuals questioning their authenticity and veracity. Debunking urban legends serves a vital role in dispelling misinformation and promoting critical thinking. Shedding light on the origins, sources, and cultural backgrounds of these legends helps us appreciate them as cultural artifacts rather than absolute truths. By understanding the various psychological and sociocultural factors that contribute to their allure, we can engage with urban legends in a more informed and critical manner. Debunking urban legends empowers individuals to navigate the intricate web of fact and fiction, fostering a more nuanced understanding of the stories that captivate us.

The Enduring Allure of Urban Legends

Urban legends continue to captivate and intrigue us, transcending time and cultural boundaries. Their ability to tap into universal human experiences, exploit psychological biases, and reflect cultural anxieties ensures their enduring appeal. As we navigate an ever-changing world, the allure of urban legends reminds us of the power of storytelling and the importance of critically engaging with narratives that shape our understanding of reality. By exploring the multidimensional nature of urban legends, we can uncover profound insights into the collective human psyche, enrich our cultural understanding, and embrace the enduring fascination that these captivating stories evoke.

The impact of urban legends on society

One of the significant ways urban legends impact society is through the dissemination of misinformation. Urban legends often contain elements of truth blended with fabrication, which can make it challenging to discern fact from fiction. As these narratives circulate among individuals, they can become accepted as truth or influence people's beliefs, leading to the spread of misinformation. This impact is particularly significant in the age of the internet, where urban legends can quickly go viral and be shared across various online platforms, reaching a wide audience. Misinformation perpetuated by urban legends can have serious consequences, influencing public sentiment, shaping political beliefs, or even affecting health-related decisions.

Furthermore, urban legends can also shape societal perceptions and behavior by fostering a sense of fear and anxiety. Many urban legends exploit common fears, such as the fear of the unknown, danger, or supernatural elements. These narratives tap into deep-rooted psychological factors, triggering responses of fear and caution. As people hear or read these legends, they may become more apprehensive about certain situations or places, altering their behavior accordingly. For example, a well-known urban legend involving a dangerous creature may cause individuals to avoid certain areas at night, even if there is no factual evidence to support the legend. This fear-induced behavior can impact the way people navigate and interact within their urban environments.

In addition to fear, urban legends also have the power to shape societal beliefs and values. Many legends often carry moral or social messages, reflecting the values and concerns of the community from which they originate. These narratives can serve as cautionary tales or reinforce social norms, thereby impacting the actions and choices of individuals. For instance, an urban legend warning against the dangers of hitchhiking may lead individuals to avoid this activity altogether, even if statistical data suggests that it is relatively safe. Thus, urban legends can influence individuals' perceptions of risk and shape their behaviors accordingly, reinforcing societal values and norms.

Despite the potentially negative impact of urban legends, they also serve as a means of entertainment and cultural bonding. These narratives provide a shared experience among individuals who hear or retell them, creating a sense of community and connection. Urban legends often circulate among friends, family, or coworkers, serving as topics of conversation and social bonding. In this sense, urban legends contribute to the formation of social networks and provide a common cultural currency. They spark curiosity, encourage storytelling, and allow individuals to engage with narratives that capture their imagination, providing entertainment and a platform for collective social engagement.

Furthermore, the study and analysis of urban legends offer insights into societal fears, anxieties, and desires. The themes and motifs present in urban legends often reflect and respond to the concerns of a particular time and place. By studying these narratives, researchers can gain a deeper understanding of the collective psyche and cultural climate of a society. For example, an abundance of urban legends in a particular community surrounding a fear of strangers may reflect prevalent issues of crime and safety in that area. By examining urban legends, researchers can explore the socio-cultural dynamics of a society and identify important social, political, and psychological trends. These narratives can lead to the dissemination of misinformation, shape perceptions and behavior through fear and anxiety, influence societal beliefs and values, provide entertainment and cultural bonding, and offer insights into the collective psyche of a society. Recognizing the potential impact of urban legends allows us to critically analyze and question the narratives we encounter, helping us navigate a world where fact and fiction can often blur. By understanding the power and influence of urban legends, we can better grasp their significance in shaping our society and our individual lives.

Chapter 2: The Hookman Legend

ORIGINS OF THE HOOKMAN story

To understand the origins of the Hookman story, we must first recognize that urban legends often serve as cautionary tales with moral lessons. These legends are frequently created or adapted to warn people about potential dangers or societal fears. The Hookman story is no exception, as it taps into the anxieties and concerns of teenagers and parents alike. It warns against the perils of engaging in risky behavior, such as parking in secluded areas and partaking in intimate encounters. By portraying the antagonist as a disfigured and dangerous individual, the story seeks to dissuade young people from venturing into dangerous situations.

While the specific narrative of the Hookman story may have changed over time, the concept of a malevolent figure with a hook for a hand can be traced back to various mythologies and folktales. Tales of one-handed characters or creatures have been passed down through generations in different cultures worldwide. These tales often portray characters with deformities or physical impairments as symbols of danger or foreboding. Such representations may stem from the instinctive human fear of the unknown and the unfamiliar, as well as the association of physical abnormalities with evil or supernatural powers.

In the Western world, the origins of the Hookman story can be linked to the rise of urban legends and the emergence of horror themes in popular culture during the 20th century. The story gained significant traction in the United States in the mid-20th century, with variations of the narrative appearing in newspapers, radio broadcasts, and later, movies and television shows. The Hookman story quickly became a staple of campfire tales and slumber party lore, perpetuated by thrill-seekers and storytellers looking to scare their peers.

It is important to note that the Hookman story is not solely an American phenomenon. Similar tales exist in other cultures, albeit with their unique variations. For instance, in Japanese folklore, the concept of a malevolent being lurking in the dark can be found in the form of yokai or yurei. These supernatural creatures often possess disfigured features and prey on unsuspecting individuals, drawing parallels to the Hookman story. Across the globe, in South Africa, the story of "The Hook in the Door Handle" bears striking resemblances to the Western iteration, highlighting the global appeal and universality of this enduring legend.

In recent years, the Hookman story has evolved with the advent of modern technology and the rise of online platforms. Creepypastas, fictional horror stories shared on the internet, have breathed new life into the legend, allowing it to reach wider audiences and undergo further reinterpretation. These online iterations often incorporate elements of contemporary culture, such as social media or technology, to make the narrative more relatable to younger generations. The ability of the story to adapt and transcend traditional storytelling mediums is a testament to its enduring appeal. Rooted in universal fears and cautionary themes, this urban legend has captivated and frightened audiences worldwide for decades. As it continues to evolve and adapt to new storytelling mediums, the Hookman story serves as a reminder of the enduring power of folklore and the human fascination with the macabre. Whether encountered around a campfire or shared in online forums, this chilling tale persists, inviting both curiosity and trepidation.

Variations of the Hookman legend

The Hookman legend is one of the most enduring and chilling urban legends that has captured the imagination of people worldwide. As with any folk tale or myth, this tale has evolved over time and has given rise to numerous variations across different cultures and regions. This essay aims to explore some of the most notable variations of the Hookman legend, shedding light on the similarities and differences between them. By examining these different renditions, we can gain a deeper understanding of the universal themes and underlying fears that the Hookman legend taps into.

One of the most well-known variations of the Hookman legend originates from the United States, specifically around the 1950s. In this version of the story, a young couple is parked in a secluded lover's lane when they hear a news report describing an escaped mental patient with a hook for a hand. Terrified, the couple decides to leave the area but soon discovers a scratching sound on the roof of the car. Panic-stricken, they speed away and upon reaching safety find a bloody hook dangling from the car door handle. This variation of the legend capitalizes on the fear of danger lurking in the darkness of isolated places and the vulnerability that young lovers may feel when engaged in intimate activities.

In Japan, a variation of the Hookman legend known as "Katakirauwa" has gained popularity. According to this version, a vengeful spirit of a woman who was gruesomely slain by her lover seeks revenge on unsuspecting couples in isolated areas. Instead of a hook, the spirit manifests as a disfigured hand with long, sharp nails. Similar to other renditions, the Katakirauwa legend maintains the backdrop of lovers parked in secluded areas, highlighting the dangers of intimacy and the potential consequences of illicit relationships. This variation, however, introduces a supernatural element, playing on traditional Japanese ghost stories and beliefs.

Moving to Latin America, the Hookman legend takes a different form, but the underlying themes of fear and caution remain intact. In Mexico, for instance, there is a variation known as "El Gancho." This legend tells the story of a deranged man who lost his hand in a violent accident and replaced it with a large hook. The Hookman, driven by a deep hatred for promiscuity and infidelity, roams the streets at night searching for unfaithful partners to punish. Unlike other versions, this rendition focuses more on moral lessons and the punishment of immoral behavior. It serves as a cautionary tale, warning against unfaithfulness and the potentially dire consequences it may bring.

While the variations of the Hookman legend may differ in their cultural and regional contexts, they all share common elements that underscore universal human fears. The isolated lovers' setting creates a sense of vulnerability and helplessness, tapping into the fear of being attacked when least expected. The inclusion of a disfigured limb, whether it is a hook or a deformed hand, intensifies the horror. These physical deformities symbolize both the monstrous nature of the antagonist and the potential consequences of indulging in taboo behaviors.

The Hookman legend, in all of its variations, serves as a cautionary tale, reminding us of the dangers that may lurk around us and the importance of being vigilant in unfamiliar or isolated settings. It taps into our deepest fears, reminding us of the fragility of life and the consequences of our actions. Despite the variations across different cultures, the Hookman legend remains a timeless cautionary narrative that continues to captivate and terrify audiences, reminding us always to be mindful of the darkness that resides within the shadows of our lives.

Real-life incidents related to the Hookman legend

One of the most intriguing real-life incidents related to the Hookman legend occurred in the late 1960s in a small town nestled deep within the American countryside. Sarah, a local teenager, had recently heard about the Hookman legend and considered it to be nothing more than a made-up tale designed to frighten young minds. One fateful night, she found herself on a deserted road, returning home from a late-night bonfire with friends. Suddenly, her car experienced a mechanical failure which left her stranded in the middle of nowhere. Uneasy, Sarah locked her doors, hoping for someone to pass by and offer assistance. Just as she was beginning to lose hope, she heard a faint tapping noise on her window. Reluctantly, she glanced in the side-view mirror, only to be confronted with a horrifying sight - a tall figure with a hook for a hand standing just outside her car window. Paralyzed with fear, Sarah quickly realized that the Hookman legend might not be fictional after all. Fortunately, before the figure could take any action, a car approached, scaring off the mysterious person and rescuing Sarah from a potentially horrendous fate.

Another chilling incident that echoes the Hookman legend took place more recently in a bustling city. It involved a group of college students who decided to explore a supposedly haunted area known locally as "Hookman's Hollow." These daring individuals were intrigued by the legend and eager to debunk its authenticity. Armed with cameras and curious minds, they ventured into the heart of the hollow one dark night. As they trekked further into the ominous woods, strange sounds echoed through the trees, sending shivers down their spines. Suddenly, their path was obstructed by a fallen tree, forcing them to detour through a winding and narrow trail. Nervously, they pressed on, their flashlights casting eerie shadows on the surrounding trees. Just as they were about to turn back, they stumbled upon a dilapidated cabin. Peering cautiously through the window, they spotted a hook hanging on the wall, confirming the presence of an eerie parallel to the Hookman legend. Bravely, they decided to document their findings. However, as they focused their cameras on the room, the door to the cabin slammed shut with an unnerving force. Panic ensued, and the students scrambled to escape. Though shaken by the incident, they managed to flee the cabin unharmed. To this day, it remains unclear who or what was responsible for their horrifying encounter.

While these real-life incidents related to the Hookman legend evoke a sense of terror and unease, it is essential to remember that the line between fact and fiction can sometimes blur. Is it possible that these occurrences are mere coincidences. Or is there some truth underlying the folklore, providing an inexplicable connection to these inexplicable events. Exploring these incidents raises intriguing questions and allows us to delve deeper into the power of folklore and its impact on our perceptions of reality.

The Hookman legend serves as a cautionary tale, warning individuals about the dangers that lurk in the shadows. It reminds us to remain vigilant and attentive to our surroundings, especially when embarking on unfamiliar adventures. The fact that real-life incidents have been associated with this legend only adds to its allure and the fascination it holds in popular culture.

As we conclude this one, it is vital to understand that the Hookman legend, although rooted in folklore, can resonate with our deepest fears and anxieties. Whether it is an encounter with a mysterious figure on a dark road or a startling discovery in an abandoned cabin, these incidents remind us of the universal human experience of facing the unknown. The Hookman legend, with its blend of truth and fiction, continues to captivate us, urging us to question the boundary between reality and the eerie realms of folklore.

Chapter 3: The Vanishing Hitchhiker Myth

THE POPULAR VERSIONS of the Vanishing Hitchhiker story

One of the most well-known versions of the Vanishing Hitchhiker story revolves around a lone traveler driving late at night when they encounter a young woman on the side of the road. In this version, the hitchhiker appears distressed and requests a ride home. Despite the traveler's best efforts to assist her, when they arrive at her supposed destination, she has mysteriously vanished from their car. Bewildered and unnerved, the traveler later discovers that the woman was actually a ghost who died tragically on that very road years ago.

This version of the Vanishing Hitchhiker story is a recurrent theme in urban legends of ghostly encounters. It often serves as a cautionary tale, warning individuals against picking up hitchhikers or venturing out alone in desolate areas. The appeal of this legend lies in its suspenseful narrative and supernatural elements, which tap into our primal fears of the unknown and the supernatural. It also raises intriguing questions about the afterlife and the lingering presence of spirits in our world.

However, it is important to note that the Vanishing Hitchhiker story is not confined to a single version. As with any urban legend, numerous variations have emerged over time, reflecting the cultural nuances and beliefs of different regions and communities. For instance, in some versions, the hitchhiker is a male figure, adding a different dynamic to the story. Additionally, the backstory of the ghostly hitchhiker may vary, ranging from tragic accidents to tales of murder or unrequited love.

The popularity of the Vanishing Hitchhiker story can be attributed to its ability to adapt and evolve, capturing the imagination of new generations. This legend has been passed down orally, shared among friends, and spread through books, movies, and the internet. Each retelling brings forth a unique interpretation, while still retaining the core elements that make the tale so intriguing.

In contemporary culture, the Vanishing Hitchhiker story continues to resonate, inspiring countless adaptations and references. It has been featured in literature, such as Richard Adams' "The Girl in a Swing" and Stephen King's "Riding the Bullet." The story has also made its way into films, with notable examples including the 1986 horror movie "The Hitcher" and the 2007 thriller "Dead End." These modern interpretations contribute to the ongoing popularity of the Vanishing Hitchhiker legend, ensuring its enduring presence as a captivating and chilling tale.

Beyond mere entertainment, the Vanishing Hitchhiker story holds deeper cultural significance. It serves as a cautionary tale, reminding us of the dangers of the unknown and the consequences of our actions. It reflects our collective fascination with the supernatural and the enduring belief in the existence of ghosts and spirits. In some cases, the story may also be seen as a metaphor for the transient nature of human connections, highlighting the fragility and ephemeral quality of our encounters with others. This urban legend continues to evolve and adapt, reflecting the diverse narratives and cultural beliefs of different communities. Its enduring presence in literature, film, and popular culture speaks to its timeless appeal and confirms its status as an enduring and captivating tale.

Historical background of the Vanishing Hitchhiker myth

One of the earliest documented versions of the Vanishing Hitchhiker myth can be found in European folklore, particularly in England and Ireland. During the 18th and 19th centuries, rural communities shared stories of spectral travelers who would mysteriously appear on the road, requesting a ride to a nearby destination. These tales, often shared around the fireplace on long winter nights, were intended to caution listeners about the dangers of picking up strangers. The apparitions were believed to be the souls of the deceased, seeking assistance or closure before reaching their final resting place. This blend of supernatural elements and cautionary themes laid the groundwork for the evolution of the Vanishing Hitchhiker myth.

As the myth transcended borders and traveled across the Atlantic, it found a new home in the United States. The rise of the automobile industry and the subsequent increase in road travel during the early 20th century created the perfect environment for the Vanishing Hitchhiker to flourish. American regional variations of the tale emerged, incorporating local landmarks and cultural nuances. Tales of a beautiful young woman appearing on the side of a desolate road and vanishing from a moving vehicle incited both fascination and trepidation.

The Vanishing Hitchhiker myth gained further popularity through the publication of Jan Harold Brunvand's influential book, "The Vanishing Hitchhiker: American Urban Legends and Their Meanings," in 1981. Brunvand, a folklorist and professor of English, meticulously analyzed and dissected the myth from a sociological and cultural standpoint. His work introduced the Vanishing Hitchhiker to a wider audience, placing it within the broader context of American urban legends.

Drawing on the historical background of the Vanishing Hitchhiker myth, we can also explore its underlying psychological and sociological significance. The enduring appeal of this folklore lies in its ability to tap into universal fears and anxieties, such as the fear of the unknown, the transient nature of life, and the uncertainty of death. By embodying these fears in the form of a hitchhiker, the myth serves as a cautionary tale, reminding us of the risks associated with helping strangers or venturing into unfamiliar territory.

Furthermore, the Vanishing Hitchhiker myth provides a lens into the cultural and societal values of the times in which it emerged. Its prevalence during periods of social upheaval and unrest can be seen as a reflection of a collective longing for stability and order. In times of uncertainty, myths and legends offer a means of understanding and making sense of the world, providing a semblance of control in the face of chaos. From its European folklore roots to its evolution in the American urban legends canon, this chilling tale continues to captivate and intrigue. By examining its origins and significance, we gain a deeper appreciation of the timeless appeal and enduring power of this haunting myth.

Psychological theories behind the Vanishing Hitchhiker phenomenon

The Vanishing Hitchhiker phenomenon has intrigued and captivated the minds of people for decades. It is a mysterious and anecdotal occurrence where an individual offers a ride to a hitchhiker, only for the hitchhiker to inexplicably vanish during the journey or shortly after being dropped off. This phenomenon has sparked various debates and theories, many of which stem from the realms of psychology. In this one, we will delve into the depths of the human mind, exploring psychological theories that may help shed light on this puzzling phenomenon.

One of the prominent psychological theories that can be applied to the Vanishing Hitchhiker phenomenon is the concept of collective memory. Collective memory refers to the shared beliefs, stories, and historical events passed down through generations within a culture or society. These memories can play a significant role in shaping individual behavior and perception. In the case of the Vanishing Hitchhiker, a widely known urban legend, the collective memory surrounding the story may contribute to its perpetuation.

The power of storytelling should not be underestimated when considering the psychological underpinnings of the Vanishing Hitchhiker phenomenon. Human beings are natural storytellers, and our brains are wired to respond to narratives. As individuals share their personal encounters with the Vanishing Hitchhiker, they contribute to the creation of a collective narrative. These stories evoke a sense of mystery, fear, and fascination, captivating audiences and encouraging the passing on of the legend.

From a psychological perspective, it is important to recognize the role of perception and memory in shaping our experiences and beliefs. The phenomenon may be a result of memory distortion and confirmation bias. When engaging with the Vanishing Hitchhiker story, individuals may selectively recall details that align with the narrative, while disregarding or forgetting contradictory information. This cognitive bias reinforces the belief in the phenomenon, as memories become reinforced through shared anecdotes and storytelling.

Furthermore, cognitive dissonance may play a part in the perpetuation of the Vanishing Hitchhiker phenomenon. Cognitive dissonance arises when an individual holds conflicting beliefs or values. In the case of encountering a vanishing hitchhiker, individuals may experience a dissonance between their belief in the paranormal or supernatural and their rational understanding of the physical world. This dissonance can be resolved by embracing the mysterious and unexplained nature of the phenomenon, allowing individuals to maintain both their belief in the supernatural and their adherence to rationality.

Another aspect to consider is the psychological need for certainty and control. Humans have an innate desire to make sense of the world and to feel a sense of control over their lives. The Vanishing Hitchhiker challenges this need by presenting an event that defies explanation. This psychological need for certainty and control may drive individuals to seek answers and create theories that provide a sense of understanding and order. But in the case of the Vanishing Hitchhiker, certainty may remain elusive, fueling further intrigue and fascination.

The psychological theory of cognitive biases also offers insights into why the Vanishing Hitchhiker phenomenon continues to thrive. Confirmation bias, as mentioned earlier, can influence the way individuals interpret and remember information that confirms their preexisting beliefs. In the case of the Vanishing Hitchhiker, individuals who already believe in the paranormal are more likely to embrace and share stories that align with their beliefs, while dismissing or downplaying alternative explanations. This biases the available evidence in favor of the phenomenon, perpetuating its existence.

To recapitulate, social psychology can shed light on the role of social influence in shaping belief systems and perpetuating legends such as the Vanishing Hitchhiker. Through a process known as pluralistic ignorance, individuals may conform to the beliefs and behaviors of a group, even if they personally hold different views. When surrounded by others who believe in the Vanishing Hitchhiker phenomenon, individuals may internalize these beliefs to fit in or avoid disapproval. The power of social influence contributes to the popularity and persistence of the phenomenon.

The Vanishing Hitchhiker phenomenon is a captivating topic that bridges the worlds of folklore, psychology, and human behavior. Through the lens of various psychological theories, we can begin to understand the complexities that underlie this mysterious occurrence. From collective memory and storytelling to cognitive biases and social influence, these psychological factors interact and contribute to the perpetuation of the Vanishing Hitchhiker legend, ensuring its presence in our cultural consciousness for years to come.

Chapter 4: The Bloody Mary Curse

THE HISTORY OF THE Bloody Mary ritual

To truly understand the history of the Bloody Mary ritual, we must first examine its origins. The Bloody Mary ritual finds its roots in an array of legends and practices. One popular belief suggests that the ritual was inspired by the vengeful spirit of Queen Mary I, also known as "Bloody Mary," who ruled England in the sixteenth century. It is said that if one were to stare into a mirror in a dimly lit room with a candle in hand, and repetitively chant "Bloody Mary" three times, her ghostly apparition would appear. This folklore blended with other legends surrounding mirror gazing and resulted in what we now know as the Bloody Mary ritual.

As time went on, the Bloody Mary ritual became a part of various cultural references and traditions. It gained popularity among children during sleepovers or gatherings as a dare or spooky game. Its inclusion in popular culture, particularly in horror movies and literature, further cemented its status as a mysterious and intriguing phenomenon. The ritual's association with the supernatural and its potential for fear and excitement made it a beloved subject in countless urban legends and campfire stories, enchanting audiences across generations.

In recent years, the Bloody Mary ritual has experienced a resurgence, with various interpretations and adaptations taking center stage. While the traditional ritual predominantly involved chanting "Bloody Mary" into a mirror, contemporary versions have emerged, introducing new elements such as using a red-tinted cocktail as a symbolic representation of the ritual's namesake. This modern twist not only adds a sense of playfulness to the ritual but also allows individuals to partake in the tradition without the fear that traditionally surrounded it.

The fascination with the Bloody Mary ritual goes beyond its supernatural associations. It is worth noting that rituals, in general, have long played an essential role in human history and culture. Rituals are deeply rooted in our need for order, structure, and symbolic representation. They provide a sense of purpose, meaning, and connection to something greater than ourselves. The Bloody Mary ritual, with its historical background and cultural significance, taps into these innate human desires, offering a glimpse into the realm of the unknown while simultaneously serving as a source of entertainment and communal experience.

In analyzing the history of the Bloody Mary ritual, it is evident that its allure lies in its ability to evoke curiosity, fear, and fascination simultaneously. Its roots in folklore and superstition, combined with its place in popular culture, lend the ritual an intriguing mystique. Furthermore, its adaptability and modern interpretations ensure its continued relevance in contemporary society.

As we conclude this one, we can appreciate the lasting power and enduring appeal of the Bloody Mary ritual. From its ancient beginnings to its modern-day variations, this ritual has intrigued and enthralled individuals across time and cultures. Its historical significance, cultural references, and contemporary adaptations form a tapestry that both captivates and perplexes. The Bloody Mary ritual continues to be a testament to the human fascination with the unknown, acting as a reminder of our shared fascination with ritual and the stories that surround them.

Different interpretations of the Bloody Mary legend

One interpretation of the Bloody Mary legend revolves around a supernatural entity or spirit. According to this interpretation, if you stand alone in front of a mirror in a dark room and repeat the name "Bloody Mary" three times, the spirit of a vengeful woman will appear. It is believed that this spirit is the ghost of the real-life Queen Mary I, seeking revenge for the crimes committed against her during her reign. This interpretation often evokes fear and is popular among those who enjoy the thrill of supernatural narratives.

Another interpretation of the Bloody Mary legend focuses on the psychological aspects of the tale. In this version, the appearance of Bloody Mary in the mirror is seen as a manifestation of one's own fears and anxieties. By repeating "Bloody Mary" three times, individuals are essentially summoning their own darkest thoughts and inviting them to take form in the mirror. This interpretation suggests that the legend serves as a metaphor for facing and conquering one's inner demons, making it a thought-provoking and introspective take on the legend.

Some interpretations of the Bloody Mary legend shift the focus from a vengeful spirit or personal fears to a cautionary tale. In these versions, the legend is often used to warn children against engaging in activities that may bring harm or undesirable consequences. The act of summoning Bloody Mary in the mirror is viewed as a dangerous and forbidden action, representing the temptations in life that should be avoided. This interpretation aims to impart a moral lesson to young audiences, encouraging them to make wise choices and think about the potential consequences of their actions.

Alternatively, the Bloody Mary legend has also been interpreted as a form of societal critique. In this view, the tale reflects the limitations and oppression faced by women throughout history. Queen Mary I, who is associated with the legend, ruled during a time when women's power was often undermined or outright denied. By embracing the character of Bloody Mary, individuals may be reclaiming this historical figure and using her legend as a means of empowerment. This interpretation recognizes the struggle of women to assert themselves and challenges the traditional narratives that have marginalized them.

It is important to note that interpretations of the Bloody Mary legend can vary significantly depending on cultural, regional, and personal beliefs. These interpretations are not mutually exclusive, and individuals may hold different views at different times or in different contexts. Whether it is seen as a spooky supernatural encounter or a metaphorical exploration of the self, the diverse interpretations of the Bloody Mary legend have contributed to its enduring popularity and continued fascination. It has been interpreted as a supernatural encounter, a psychological exploration, a cautionary tale, and a critique of societal norms. Regardless of the specific interpretation, the legend continues to inspire curiosity and provoke thought, making it a timeless and fascinating subject for discussion and study.

The science behind the Bloody Mary curse

Often told during slumber parties and around campfires, this supernatural tale involves summoning a vengeful spirit named Bloody Mary, known for her eerie appearances in mirrors. While the legend has passed down through generations, this exploration aims to delve into the science behind the Bloody Mary curse, seeking a rational explanation for the seemingly paranormal occurrences associated with this haunting tale.

1. The Power of Imagination and Suggestion:

To understand the science behind the Bloody Mary curse, we first need to acknowledge the power of imagination and suggestion. Psychologists have long recognized that our mind's ability to create vivid mental images can have a profound impact on our perception and behavior. When individuals gather in anticipation of summoning Bloody Mary, their minds become primed for a potentially eerie encounter. This heightened state allows their imaginations to run wild, making them more susceptible to even the faintest signals or cues that might confirm their beliefs.

2. The Role of Mirror Gazing:

Central to the Bloody Mary legend is the act of mirror gazing. This activity, involving prolonged visual engagement with one's reflection, has been associated with altered states of consciousness and even hallucinations. The phenomenon of "scrying," in which individuals attempt to glimpse the supernatural through mirrors, dates back centuries and continues to captivate our collective imagination. Mirror gazing, coupled with the suggestive atmosphere created during the summoning ritual, can induce a heightened state of suggestibility and amplify any perceptual experiences, further blurring the line between reality and imagination.

3. The Ideomotor Effect:

One significant factor contributing to the eerie experiences associated with the Bloody Mary curse is the ideomotor effect. This psychological phenomenon refers to the involuntary and unconscious muscle movements that occur in response to an individual's thoughts and beliefs. When someone believes they are summoning Bloody Mary, the mind's suggestion can trigger subtle physical movements, such as trembling hands or a slight shift in body posture. These actions, while seemingly involuntary, are intricately linked to our mental state and can create the illusion of supernatural phenomena.

4. The Impact of Low Light Conditions:

Another crucial element in the Bloody Mary curse is the dim or dark conditions usually employed during its performance. Research has shown that low light conditions can significantly impact our perception, leading to visual distortions and misinterpretations. Coupled with heightened suggestibility, this setting can enhance the perceived supernatural elements in mirror gazing experiences. Shadows, reflections, and the brain's tendency to seek familiarity in random patterns can all contribute to the eerie sensations often reported during attempts to summon Bloody Mary.

5. Cultural and Social Conditioning:

The power of cultural and social conditioning cannot be overlooked when discussing the science behind the Bloody Mary curse. From an early age, individuals are exposed to tales and anecdotes surrounding this legend, shaping their expectations of what to anticipate during the summoning ritual. As cultural norms and shared beliefs influence our perception and interpretation of events, it is no surprise that those familiar with the story are more likely to experience sensations associated with the curse than those who are not.

WHILE THE BLOODY MARY curse may continue to captivate our imaginations and send shivers down our spines, delving into its scientific underpinnings can provide a rational perspective on this haunting tale. From the power of suggestion and mirror gazing to the ideomotor effect, low light conditions, and cultural conditioning, numerous psychological and perceptual factors contribute to the eerie experiences associated with this legend. By understanding these scientific aspects, we can appreciate how our minds and environment play a significant role in shaping our encounters with the seemingly supernatural.

Chapter 5: The Slender Man Myth

THE ORIGINS OF THE Slender Man myth

The tale of the Slender Man begins in the decade following the turn of the 21st century, predominantly on internet forums dedicated to horror and spooky stories. It was in 2009 that the Slender Man first emerged on the Something Awful forums, a platform known for fostering creative and often eerie discussions. Eric Knudsen, also known by his online pseudonym "Victor Surge," posted two photographs he had manipulated to include a tall, faceless figure lurking in the background. Accompanying these images, Knudsen crafted a fictional backstory that spoke of a supernatural entity haunting children and driving them to madness or disappearance.

These posts sparked a wave of interest and creativity among the online community, leading to an explosion of Slender Man lore. Hordes of contributors constructed their own stories, images, and videos, building upon the mythos established by Knudsen. This collaborative storytelling approach allowed for an ever-expanding universe around the Slender Man, with each addition contributing to the collective canon. The interactive nature of these contributions not only fueled the myth's growth but also blurred the lines between reality and fiction.

However, it is essential to recognize that the Slender Man myth did not emerge in a cultural vacuum. The origins draw on deep-seated human fears and folklore dating back centuries. The notion of a menacing, faceless presence haunting forests and preying on those who dare to venture into its domain echoes in folklore across different cultures. From the shadowy figures depicted in German woodcuts to the "Men in Black" found in international legends, the archetype of a foreboding entity has long captivated our collective psyche.

Furthermore, the influence of various media, both ancient and modern, can be traced within the framework of the Slender Man myth. The work of horror writer H.P. Lovecraft, with his concept of cosmic horror and otherworldly figures, bears notable similarities to the Slender Man's unsettling presence and unknown origins. Lovecraft's influence can be seen in the way Slender Man lurks at the fringes of human understanding, leaving only fragmented clues and instilling a sense of cosmic dread.

As time went on, the Slender Man mythos permeated different media platforms, with creators exploring the concept in both fiction and documentary forms. Independent video games like "Slender: The Eight Pages" brought the myth into the realm of interactive horror, amplifying its reach and immersing players in the eerie world of the Slender Man. The advent of social media further accelerated the dissemination of the myth, allowing for the instant sharing of stories, images, and videos, thus heightening its presence and popularity.

However, the prominence of the Slender Man myth took a chilling turn when the character became the center of a real-life tragedy. In 2014, two 12-year-old girls in Wisconsin lured a classmate to the woods, where they stabbed her 19 times, claiming that they committed the gruesome act to appease the Slender Man. This shocking incident brought the Slender Man myth to mainstream attention, raising debates about the influence of online content and the boundaries between fiction and reality.

It is crucial to note that the intentions behind the Slender Man myth were never malicious or intended to incite violence. Yet, this real-world incident forced a broader conversation about the responsibility of creators and consumers of online content. It highlighted how individuals, particularly those with pre-existing vulnerabilities, may interpret and act upon fictional narratives.

Despite this horrific event, the Slender Man myth continues to evolve and capture the imagination of people around the world. Various adaptations and reinterpretations in literature, film, and other creative mediums continuously breathe new life into the narrative. This ongoing evolution underscores the enduring power of ancient folklore combined with the collaborative nature of online storytelling, giving rise to a modern myth that resonates deeply with our cultural anxieties and desires for the unexplained. What began as an online forum post morphed into a vast universe of unnerving tales, videos, and images that continue to captivate and unsettle audiences. Combining elements of ancient folklore and the work of horror creators like H.P. Lovecraft, the Slender Man myth embodies our collective fears and fascinations. Its expansion into different media platforms and the tragic real-life event it influenced only serve to underline the powerful role storytelling plays in shaping our cultural consciousness.

The impact of the Slender Man on popular culture

One of the most striking aspects of the Slender Man's impact on popular culture is the way in which it has transcended traditional boundaries. The character's origin on the internet, specifically on the Something Awful forum, reveals how a piece of digital folklore can rapidly spread and embed itself in the collective consciousness. Through a combination of images, stories, and video series like the groundbreaking "Marble Hornets," the Slender Man mythos soon became synonymous with internet horror culture. Its viral nature enabled a wide spectrum of creators to engage with the character, leading to the development of countless spin-off stories, artwork, and fan-made content.

While the Slender Man initially gained popularity online, it did not take long for his presence to extend into other forms of media, effectively "crossing over" into mainstream popular culture. Video games like "Slender: The Eight Pages" and its subsequent adaptations capitalized on the pervasive fear the character generated, allowing players to immerse themselves in the world of the Slender Man. These games, often employing a found footage aesthetic and requiring players to navigate dark and eerie environments, caused a sensation and demonstrated the impact this cyber-mythology had on interactive entertainment.

Notably, the Slender Man also made his mark in the realm of literature. Countless self-published novels and short stories have been written about the character, expanding on his lore and exploring different aspects of his abilities and motivations. These works, while varying in quality, highlight the enduring appeal of the Slender Man as a character and the immense creative potential that he inspires. Additionally, the character has also appeared in more mainstream publications, such as R.L. Stine's "Slenderman," demonstrating how even established authors recognize the cultural significance and commercial viability of the mythos.

Perhaps the most controversial aspect of the Slender Man's impact on popular culture is the chilling way in which it seeped into real-life incidents. In 2014, two young girls in Wisconsin attempted to murder their classmate, claiming that they were motivated by the Slender Man's instructions. This shocking incident sparked widespread debate about the effect of online horror and the responsibility of media creators. It also emphasized the blurred lines between fiction and reality in the digital age. While this event was undoubtedly tragic, it serves as a stark reminder of the power of urban legends and their potential influence on vulnerable individuals.

The influence of the Slender Man on popular culture can be seen as just one example of the enduring power of folklore. Folklore, whether traditional or digital, has long played a significant role in shaping societies and providing a framework through which people interpret the world around them. The Slender Man's ability to capture the imagination and generate fear speaks to the broader human fascination with the eerie and unknown. By examining the impact of the Slender Man on popular culture, we gain valuable insights into the underlying psychological mechanisms that drive our fascination with such supernatural entities and the enduring appeal they hold for generations. From its humble beginnings as an internet meme to its expansion into various media outlets and the controversy that unfolded in real life, the Slender Man has left an indelible mark on our collective psyche. This phenomenon highlights the power of folklore, the interconnectedness of online communities, and the blurred lines between reality and fiction. The Slender Man's impact on popular culture invites us to reflect on our own fascination with the dark and unknown, and to explore the profound effects that urban legends can have on the human imagination in the digital era.

Real-life incidents influenced by the Slender Man legend

Among these legends, the haunting tale of Slender Man has undeniably captivated the imagination of people worldwide. Created on an online forum in 2009, the enigmatic figure of Slender Man has developed into a pervasive mythos. While largely existing in the realm of fiction, the Slender Man legend has had a profound impact on real-life incidents that shed light on the fascinating and sometimes unsettling power of urban legends. In this exploration, we will delve into some notable cases influenced by the Slender Man legend, analyzing their origins, repercussions, and the lessons they provide about human psychology and the pervasiveness of storytelling.

Case 1: The Slender Man Stabbing in 2014:

Undoubtedly, one of the most notorious incidents influenced by the Slender Man legend occurred in Waukesha, Wisconsin, in 2014. Two 12-year-old girls, motivated by an obsession with the fictional figure, lured a classmate into the woods and stabbed her multiple times. The victim survived, prompting a profound examination of the role of the internet, mental health, and the power of urban legends in young minds. This horrifying incident brought nationwide attention to the Slender Man phenomenon and sparked debates regarding the potential dangers of consuming and internalizing fictional narratives.

Case 2: The Sighting Reports and Mass Hysteria:

The Slender Man legend has also given rise to numerous sighting reports and episodes of mass hysteria. From random individuals claiming to have encountered the infamous figure to widespread panic in communities, these incidents illustrate the real-world consequences of a digital folklore. While some may dismiss these reports as mere fabrications or misinterpretations, they highlight the deep-rooted impact of urban legends on our collective consciousness. The manifestation of mass hysteria surrounding the Slender Man legend emphasizes the human inclination to blur the boundaries between reality and fiction, particularly in the face of fear and uncertainty.

Case 3: Slender Man in Popular Culture:

Outside the realm of actual incidents, the Slender Man legend has flourished within popular culture, solidifying its presence in various mediums. The character has been adapted into video games, films, literature, and even inspired a documentary exploring the effects of the legend's influence. This cross-pollination between the fictional and real worlds strengthens the allure of urban legends, making them ever more pervasive and deeply ingrained in our societal fabric. By analyzing these adaptations, we uncover the ways in which Slender Man has become a multimedia phenomenon and a testament to the potency of urban legends in an increasingly interconnected world.

Case 4: The Slender Man Trial:

Another notable incident linked to the Slender Man legend was the subsequent trial of the two girls involved in the 2014 stabbing case. The trial raised profound questions about culpability, mental health, and the consequences of online communities that perpetuate dark narratives. It also raised concerns about the potential impact of fictional characters on vulnerable individuals, exploring the moral and legal boundaries of responsibility for acts committed under the influence of imaginary figures. The trial's outcome, which involved a focus on the girls' mental state and the influence of the Slender Man legend, shed light on the complex relationship between fiction, reality, and culpability in contemporary society.

THE INFLUENCE OF THE Slender Man legend on real-life incidents exemplifies the power of urban legends to shape perceptions, actions, and even legal proceedings. From the harrowing stabbing case to mass hysteria and the cultural adaptations, these incidents underscore the significance of studying the impact of such legends on individuals and society as a whole. They teach us valuable lessons about the blurred lines between fiction and reality, the susceptibility of human psychology to gripping narratives, and the need for responsible storytelling in an age of instant information exchange. As we navigate the intricate interplay of legends and their consequences, it is crucial to recognize the potential influence urban legends can wield, both for better and for worse, in our ever-evolving world.

Chapter 6: The Babysitter and the Man Upstairs Tale

HISTORICAL BACKGROUND of the Babysitter and the Man Upstairs legend

The origins of the Babysitter and the Man Upstairs legend, like many urban legends, are shrouded in mystery and ambiguity. While it is challenging to pinpoint the exact source or earliest recorded version of the story, its widespread circulation can be attributed to the oral tradition and the subsequent proliferation of mass media. It is believed that this legend emerged in the mid-20th century, coinciding with the rise of suburban America and the increasing prevalence of teenagers taking on babysitting jobs.

The 1950s and 1960s witnessed a significant societal shift as the American suburbs experienced rapid growth. With more families living in these residential areas, the demand for babysitters rose, providing ample opportunities for teenagers to earn money and gain independence. However, this newfound freedom and responsibility also exposed young babysitters to potential dangers. The Babysitter and the Man Upstairs legend tapped into the fears and anxieties associated with this vulnerable position, highlighting the potential risks of being alone in someone else's home.

During this time, advancements in telephone technology also played a crucial role in the legend's development. The advent of direct-dialing and increased accessibility to telephone lines added a new dimension to the suspense and terror of the story. The sound of a ringing phone, once a symbol of communication and connection, became a source of dread and alarm for babysitters who found themselves in dangerous situations. The legend exploited this technological advancement, emphasizing the threat that could be lurking just a phone call away.

The legend's depiction of the Man Upstairs as the embodiment of evil represents a broader cultural fear that predates the specific narrative. Throughout history, various tales and myths have explored the notion of a malevolent being residing in the upper levels of a building. From Gothic literature to psychological thrillers, this motif has been used to create a sense of unease and suspense. The role of the Man Upstairs in the Babysitter legend amplifies the fear of the unknown, as the babysitter navigates the dark, unfamiliar territory of someone else's home.

As time progressed, the Babysitter and the Man Upstairs legend continued to evolve and adapt to the changing social landscape. The gratification of witnessing a female protagonist triumph over an evil antagonist resonated with audiences and contributed to the legend's enduring popularity. Additionally, the legend's cautionary undertones served as a reminder to young babysitters and their families of the importance of vigilance and safety precautions.

The impact and cultural significance of the Babysitter and the Man Upstairs legend are evident in its continued presence in contemporary popular culture. Its themes and elements have been referenced and reimagined in numerous movies, books, and television shows, further solidifying its status as an enduring urban legend. The tale's ability to tap into primal fears and examine the vulnerabilities of adolescence continues to captivate audiences, ensuring its place in the pantheon of horror folklore. Emerging during the suburban boom of the mid-20th century, the legend capitalized on the fears and vulnerability of teenage babysitters. The fusion of technological advancements, such as increasingly accessible telephone lines, and the age-old trope of a malevolent presence residing upstairs contributed to the legend's enduring impact. Its cautionary nature and examination of the dangers lurking within the familiar setting of someone else's home struck a chord with audiences then and now. As urban folklore, the Babysitter and the Man Upstairs legend continues to terrify, making its mark on popular culture and ensuring its place in the ever-evolving tapestry of fear and imagination.

Similar stories from around the world

Throughout history, stories have served as a fundamental means of communication, passing down knowledge, values, and cultural aspects from one generation to another. In every corner of the globe, people have crafted tales that reflect their unique experiences, beliefs, and traditions. These stories may differ in details and characters, but they often share underlying themes and motifs that resonate across cultures. By examining similar stories from around the world, we gain valuable insights into the shared human experience and recognize the power of storytelling as a universal tool for connection and understanding.

One common theme that appears recurrently in stories from diverse cultures is the hero's journey. This archetype, popularized by Joseph Campbell in his book "The Hero with a Thousand Faces," outlines the hero's path of challenges, self-discovery, and ultimate triumph. While the specific details may vary, this universal narrative of the hero's journey can be found in numerous ancient myths, fairy tales, and epics from different cultures.

For instance, the Greek myth of Odysseus embarking on a long and perilous journey home after the Trojan War shares striking similarities to the Hindu epic of Ramayana, which recounts the journey of Prince Rama to rescue his wife Sita from the clutches of the demon king Ravana. Both stories follow the protagonists' trials, encounters with mythical creatures, and tests of their character. These parallel narratives suggest that the hero's journey resonates deeply with human aspirations and provides a standard structure for the exploration of personal growth and transformation.

Another common story motif found in various cultures is the flood myth. The tale of a catastrophic deluge sent by the gods to punish humanity is found in ancient Mesopotamian, Indian, Chinese, and Native American folklore, among others. In the Mesopotamian Epic of Gilgamesh, the hero Utnapishtim is instructed by the gods to build a massive boat to survive a cataclysmic flood. Similarly, in the biblical story of Noah's Ark, God instructs Noah to construct an ark to save himself, his family, and a pair of each animal species from the impending flood.

This shared motif of a great flood, often associated with divine wrath and subsequent rebirth or renewal, demonstrates a collective human fascination with natural disasters and their capacity for both destruction and regeneration.

It also highlights our enduring belief in the importance of redemption and second chances.

Furthermore, the motif of star-crossed lovers transcends cultural boundaries and appears in numerous stories worldwide. Shakespeare's Romeo and Juliet is perhaps the most well-known iteration of this theme, as it tells the tragic tale of two young lovers from feuding families. However, similar stories can be found in other cultural traditions.

In India, the myth of Mirza-Sahiban recounts the forbidden love between Mirza, a Muslim warrior, and Sahiban, a Punjabi princess from a rival clan. Despite their deep affection, their love is forbidden, and tragedy befalls them. In the Chinese legend of the Butterfly Lovers, two students, Liang Shanbo and Zhu Yingtai, fall deeply in love but are tragically separated by circumstances. These stories, along with countless others, demonstrate that the anguish and yearning associated with forbidden love are universal emotions that transcend cultural boundaries.

By exploring the commonalities amongst stories from around the world, we not only gain a deeper appreciation for the richness and diversity of human cultures but also recognize the underlying threads that connect us all. Through storytelling, we find common ground and build bridges of understanding that foster empathy, tolerance, and appreciation for our shared humanity. Despite the cultural, geographical, and chronological distances that separate us, similar narratives can be found across diverse cultures. Whether it is the hero's journey, the flood myth, or the tale of star-crossed lovers, these motifs speak to our collective human experiences and aspirations. By studying and appreciating these similarities, we not only gain a deeper understanding of our shared human experience but also foster a sense of connection and empathy across cultures. Storytelling truly is a universal language that transcends borders and unites us in our quest for knowledge, meaning, and connection.

The moral lessons behind the Babysitter and the Man Upstairs tale

One of the main moral lessons of this story is the significance of personal safety. The Babysitter and the Man Upstairs tale serves as a reminder that individuals should always prioritize their well-being and take necessary precautions. The babysitter in the story learns the hard way that danger can be closer than expected, even within the seemingly safe confines of a home. This tale emphasizes the need for individuals to be aware of their surroundings, trust their instincts, and take appropriate actions to protect themselves.

Another vital lesson conveyed by this infamous story is the importance of trust and the implications of misplaced trust. In the Babysitter and the Man Upstairs tale, the babysitter initially trusts that the mysterious phone calls are harmless and fails to recognize the potential danger. This decision results in dire consequences. The tale highlights the need to exercise caution when creating trust with others, especially in unfamiliar or uncertain situations. It encourages individuals to be discerning and to establish trust gradually, based on reliable evidence and clear indicators of safety.

Moreover, the Babysitter and the Man Upstairs tale offers a cautionary lesson about the need to remain vigilant. The babysitter's failure to take immediate action upon receiving the strange phone calls illustrates the concept of complacency and its potential consequences. This story underscores the importance of staying attentive, observing even minor details, and promptly addressing potential threats or red flags. By being vigilant, individuals can potentially prevent or mitigate the impact of dangerous situations.

In addition to personal safety, trust, and vigilance, this story also raises awareness about the potential dangers of technology and how it can be misused. The advent of telephones plays a crucial role in this tale, with the babysitter receiving unsettling calls that gradually become more threatening. This cautionary aspect of the story serves as a reminder that technology, while often advantageous, can also be manipulated or abused by individuals with ill intentions. It prompts us to consider the potential risks associated with our ever-increasing reliance on technology and the importance of exercising caution in its use.

While the Babysitter and the Man Upstairs tale is undoubtedly suspenseful and chilling, it offers valuable life lessons for individuals of all ages. By examining the story's underlying moral messages of personal safety, trust, vigilance, and the potential dangers of technology, we can better equip ourselves and our loved ones to navigate the complexities of the modern world. This tale serves as a vivid reminder to be cautious, remain attentive, and make informed decisions to ensure our own safety and wellbeing. By learning from the moral lessons presented in this captivating story, we can strive to create a safer and more secure environment for ourselves and those around us.

Chapter 7: The Mothman Prophecies

THE MOTHMAN SIGHTINGS in Point Pleasant, West Virginia

The town became the eerie playground for the sightings of a mysterious creature that would be later dubbed the Mothman. The Mothman sightings, which captivated the nation's attention, drew the curious and the skeptical alike to this small Appalachian town. This book aims to delve into this intriguing phenomenon, exploring eyewitness accounts, examining possible explanations, and shedding light on the enduring legacy of the Mothman.

Setting the Stage

To understand the Mothman sightings, we must first get acquainted with the rich history and unique geological features of Point Pleasant. Nestled between the Ohio and Kanawha rivers, this idyllic town was the perfect backdrop for a flurry of anomalous events. We'll explore the town's connection to Native American folklore, the significance of the nearby McClintic Wildlife Management Area, and the narratives of the local residents, whose lives were forever changed by their encounters with the Mothman.

The Myth Takes Flight

The catalyst for the Mothman legend can be traced back to November 12, 1966, when five men reported encountering a large, winged creature near the McClintic Wildlife Management Area. Word of this mysterious creature quickly spread, with subsequent sightings over the next year becoming increasingly frequent. This one will delve into the initial accounts and examine the similarities and differences among eyewitness testimony. We'll also explore how media coverage, far and wide, transformed these sightings into a full-fledged phenomenon.

Anatomy of the Mothman

Building upon the witness accounts, let's endeavor to understand the Mothman itself. What were its distinguishing features. How did witnesses describe its behavior and movements. Drawing from a multitude of testimonies, we will develop a composite sketch of this enigmatic creature. We'll also consider possible explanations for its strange appearance, including theories related to bird species, misidentified animals, and even supernatural entities.

The Terror Unleashed

As fear and speculation took hold, Point Pleasant experienced an unprecedented sense of unease. Beyond the Mothman sightings, residents began to report strange occurrences and unsettling phenomena. This one will delve into these chilling incidents, including the collapse of the Silver Bridge that claimed the lives of 46 people. We'll explore the alleged connections between the Mothman and this tragic event, evaluating the credibility and exploring alternative explanations.

The Aftermath and Legacy

Following the fallout from the Silver Bridge disaster, the Mothman sightings gradually dwindled. However, Point Pleasant could never fully escape the specter of the Mothman. In this one, we'll unravel the enduring legacy of this phenomenon. We'll delve into the cultural impact, ranging from the town's annual Mothman Festival to its appearance in popular culture through books, movies, and documentaries. Furthermore, we'll explore how the sightings of the Mothman have impacted belief systems, paranormal investigations, and the quest for answers in the larger mysterious world.

THE MOTHMAN SIGHTINGS in Point Pleasant, West Virginia, remain one of the most captivating mysteries in modern American folklore. Through eyewitness accounts, expert analysis, and a comprehensive exploration of the historical context, this book has sought to shed light on this enigma. While the ultimate truth behind the Mothman may forever elude us, the enduring fascination and desire for answers continue to drive our collective curiosity. Let us embark on this journey together, delving into the heart of a small town and its extraordinary encounters with the unknown.

Theories about the real identity of the Mothman

One theory that has gained popularity among enthusiasts is the notion that the Mothman is a supernatural or mythical being. Supporters of this theory believe that the creature is a harbinger of doom or a warning sign of impending catastrophe. They argue that the Mothman's appearance just before the tragic collapse of the Silver Bridge in 1967, which resulted in the loss of 46 lives, is evidence of its supernatural nature. According to this interpretation, the Mothman acts as a messenger, signaling impending disaster and thus serving as a cautionary figure.

Another widely discussed theory is that the Mothman is an extraterrestrial entity or an alien. Extraterrestrial enthusiasts believe that the creature is a visitor from another planet or dimension, sent to Earth to observe humans or carry out undisclosed missions. They argue that the Mothman's physical attributes, such as its wings and glowing red eyes, are characteristic of beings from outer space. This theory finds support in accounts of alleged UFO sightings coinciding with Mothman appearances. These sightings are often described as glowing orbs or unidentified flying objects, suggesting a possible extraterrestrial connection.

Taking a more grounded approach, some researchers propose psychological explanations for the Mothman phenomenon. These explanations delve into the realms of human perception, cognitive biases, and collective hysteria. According to this line of thought, the Mothman sightings could be a result of misperception, hallucination, or even mass hysteria. They argue that during times of fear, anxiety, or heightened collective consciousness, individuals are more prone to interpret vague stimuli as supernatural beings or otherworldly entities. In this context, the Mothman could be seen as a product of suggestion, fueled by the power of belief.

It is essential to approach these theories with an open mind and a critical eye. While supernatural, extraterrestrial, and psychological explanations offer some possible interpretations, none can be definitively proven or disproven. The mystery surrounding the real identity of the Mothman persists, leaving room for endless speculation and debate. Ultimately, the truth or falsehood of these theories may remain elusive, adding to the allure and fascination of this legendary creature.

Regardless of the theories surrounding the Mothman's identity, it is undeniable that the creature has left an enduring impact on popular culture. Its mythos has inspired books, movies, and even a dedicated festival in Point Pleasant. The Mothman's enduring presence in folklore and popular imagination attests to the lasting power of mysterious and unexplained phenomena. Whether one believes in the supernatural, extraterrestrial, or psychological explanations, the Mothman serves as a reminder that the unknown can captivate our collective curiosity and spark our imaginations. It is through exploring such mysteries that we expand our understanding of the world and ourselves. Theories about its true identity span from supernatural and otherworldly interpretations to psychological and cognitive explanations. Whether one believes in the Mothman as a harbinger of doom, an extraterrestrial visitor, or a product of collective imagination, its legacy endures as a testament to our fascination with the unknown. As we navigate the labyrinth of mysteries that the world presents, the allure of the Mothman and its elusive truth remind us of the tremendous breadth of human imagination and the allure of the unexplained.

The Mothman's connections to other urban legends and myths

With its glowing red eyes, enormous wingspan, and ominous presence, the Mothman has become an iconic figure in the realm of urban legends. In this one, we will explore the Mothman's connections to various other urban legends and myths, delving into the fascinating similarities and intertwined narratives that exist in the realm of folklore.

Section 1: The Mothman and Native American Folklore

The origins of the Mothman legend can be traced back to the Native American tribes of the region, particularly the Shawnee tribe. Native American folklore often contains tales of mysterious creatures and spirits that serve as harbingers or warnings. In some accounts, the Mothman is seen as a guardian of the land, a protector or omen of impending doom. Drawing parallels between the Mothman and similar legends in Native American folklore can shed light on deeper cultural and spiritual beliefs, highlighting the enduring significance of these tales across generations.

Section 2: The Mothman and Cryptids

Cryptids, creatures whose existence is unsubstantiated by mainstream science, have long intrigued enthusiasts. The Mothman belongs to this category of enigmatic beings, alongside renowned cryptids such as Bigfoot and the Loch Ness Monster. Exploring the connections between the Mothman and other cryptids, such as their shared ability to evoke fear and fascination, can help us understand the impact and enduring appeal of these urban legends within our collective consciousness.

Section 3: The Mothman and Men in Black

In the annals of urban legends, the Men in Black hold a prominent place. These mysterious figures, often described as government agents, have been associated with numerous supernatural phenomena, including UFO sightings and encounters. Curiously, reports of encounters with the Mothman are often followed by appearances of Men in Black. Unraveling the connections between the Mothman and the Men in Black can provide insights into the larger narrative of secretive government operations and the control of information.

Section 4: The Mothman and Apocalyptic Prophecies

A recurring theme within the Mothman legend is its association with catastrophic events and apocalyptic visions. Similar motifs can also be found in other legends and myths, such as tales of comets, prophecies, and signs foretelling the end of the world. By examining these connections, we can uncover the underlying human desire to decipher signs and symbols, to seek meaning in the chaos of our existence, and to grapple with the concept of mortality.

Section 5: The Mothman in Popular Culture

The influence of the Mothman transcends folklore, permeating various forms of popular culture, including books, movies, and even music. From John Keel's classic book "The Mothman Prophecies" to the 2002 film adaptation starring Richard Gere, the Mothman has woven its way into the fabric of contemporary entertainment. By exploring its impact on popular culture, we not only observe the spread of urban legends but also gain insights into how these tales shape and reflect our societal fears and desires.

THE MOTHMAN'S CONNECTIONS to other urban legends and myths offer a captivating lens through which we can explore the limitless depths of human imagination and the enduring power of folklore. By examining its ties to Native American folklore, cryptids, Men in Black, apocalyptic prophecies, and popular culture, we gain a richer understanding of the intricate tapestry of urban legends that shape our perceptions. Whether we view the Mothman as a supernatural phenomenon, a manifestation of collective fears, or a fascinating cultural phenomenon, its presence in our global consciousness is undoubtedly profound.

Chapter 8: The Black-Eyed Kids Mystery

THE FIRST REPORTED encounters with Black-Eyed Kids

The first documented encounter with Black-Eyed Kids occurred in Abilene, Texas, in the late 1990s. Brian Bethel, a journalist and eyewitness, shared his harrowing experience through an online forum, which eventually became one of the pioneering accounts of BEK encounters. According to Bethel, he was approached by two children, approximately ten to fourteen years old, who sought his help to gain entry into his vehicle. What alarmed Bethel were their entirely pitch-black eyes, devoid of any iris or whites that one would typically expect. This encounter left him shaken, and soon after, numerous other individuals began sharing similar experiences, creating a buzz around these mysterious and unsettling beings.

These encounters, remarkably consistent in their descriptions, typically involve encounters with children between the ages of six and sixteen, who exhibit peculiar behavior and possess completely black eyes. Witnesses often report feeling an overwhelming sense of dread or fear when confronted by these children. They frequently approach individuals in parking lots, residential areas, or even homes, pleading for assistance, whether it be asking for a ride, phone use, or permission to enter a property. Their insistence and persuasiveness often unnerve those who encounter them, causing an inexplicable feeling of unease.

While encounters with Black-Eyed Kids remain primarily anecdotal, several theories attempt to explain their origin and nature. One prominent theory suggests that BEKs may be supernatural entities or even extraterrestrial beings. Proponents of this theory argue that the complete absence of normal eye appearance could indicate an otherworldly or non-human nature. This theory finds support in the resemblances between BEK encounters and classic abduction narratives, where individuals are often approached or visited by mysterious beings with similar unsettling characteristics.

Another theory suggests that Black-Eyed Kids may be the result of a social or psychological phenomenon, rather than beings of a paranormal nature. Supporters of this theory argue that BEKs could be a modern manifestation of urban legends or folklore, adapted to fit the constraints of an increasingly connected and technologically advanced society. They propose that the fear and unease experienced during encounters with BEKs stem from a primal, almost evolutionary response to unfamiliar or threatening stimuli, much like the fear of the dark or the unknown.

Regardless of the theories put forth, the phenomenon of Black-Eyed Kids has unquestionably sparked the imagination of many. The reported encounters evoke a sense of both terror and fascination, leaving countless questions unanswered. Skeptics argue that these stories merely stem from a combination of misperceptions, hoaxes, and the power of suggestion. Yet, many eyewitnesses maintain their accounts, insisting that their encounters were undeniably real and profoundly unsettling. Since then, numerous accounts have emerged, describing encounters with children whose eyes are entirely black, devoid of usual iris or whites. These encounters consistently evoke intense feelings of fear and unease in witnesses, leaving an indelible mark on their psyche. While various theories attempt to explain the existence of BEKs, ranging from the supernatural to social or psychological explanations, the true nature of these unsettling beings remains shrouded in mystery. Whether one believes in the paranormal or embraces a skeptical outlook, the reports of encounters with Black-Eyed Kids continue to fascinate, perplex, and haunt the minds of those who dare to explore this enigmatic phenomenon.

Psychological explanations for the Black-Eyed Kids phenomenon

One leading psychological explanation for the Black-Eyed Kids phenomenon is rooted in the paranormal belief system known as pareidolia. Pareidolia is the natural human tendency to find meaningful patterns in ambiguous stimuli, such as seeing images in clouds or faces in objects. When encountering a Black-Eyed Kid, individuals may be experiencing a form of pareidolia, perceiving an abnormal, unsettling appearance that triggers feelings of fear or unease. This psychological predisposition to assign meaning and interpret experiences based on pre-existing beliefs and expectations can play a significant role in shaping individual responses to the phenomenon.

Another psychological explanation stems from the concept of cognitive dissonance. Cognitive dissonance occurs when individuals hold conflicting beliefs or attitudes, leading to psychological discomfort. When faced with an encounter with Black-Eyed Kids, individuals may experience cognitive dissonance due to the clash between their perception of innocence associated with children and the unsettling appearance and behavior of the Black-Eyed Kids themselves. This dissonance may result in fear and anxiety as individuals struggle to reconcile their preconceived notions of childhood with this alarming encounter, leading to a heightened emotional response.

Furthermore, the uncanny valley hypothesis, proposed by robotics professor Masahiro Mori, offers a compelling psychological explanation for the eerie and unsettling reaction individuals have towards Black-Eyed Kids. According to this hypothesis, as robots or human-like entities become more similar to real humans, there is a corresponding increase in the emotional response from observers. However, once these entities become almost indistinguishable from humans, but still exhibit subtle deviations, a significant emotional discomfort arises, causing individuals to experience fear or revulsion. The unusual appearance of Black-Eyed Kids, with their unnaturally dark-tinged eyes and lack of typical human warmth, may trigger the uncanny valley response in individuals, leading to an aversive reaction towards these beings.

In addition to these psychological explanations, the phenomenon of Black-Eyed Kids can also be understood through the lens of social psychology. Social norms play a crucial role in shaping our perception and behaviors, and encounters with Black-Eyed Kids challenge societal expectations surrounding children and their behavior. Consequently, individuals may be primed to respond with fear or caution when faced with a violation of these norms. The presence of Black-Eyed Kids who deviate from expected social behavior, combined with their eerie appearance, may activate deep-rooted protective instincts that heighten feelings of anxiety and unease in individuals.

It is essential to acknowledge that psychological explanations are not intended to dismiss or debunk personal experiences or beliefs surrounding the Black-Eyed Kids phenomenon. Instead, they provide a framework to understand the subjective experiences and emotional responses individuals have when encountering these beings. These explanations offer insights into the psychological mechanisms that may underpin the phenomenon, shedding light on the human mind's intricacies and how it constructs meaning from ambiguous encounters. From the influence of pareidolia and cognitive dissonance to the uncanny valley hypothesis and societal norms, various psychological frameworks help us better understand this eerie phenomenon. By exploring these explanations, researchers and individuals alike can continue to delve into the complexities of human perception, emotion, and belief systems, unraveling the mysteries surrounding the Black-Eyed Kids phenomenon.

How the Black-Eyed Kids legend has evolved in recent years

To understand the present-day form of the Black-Eyed Kids legend, one must delve into its origins. Although there are instances of encounters with black-eyed individuals dating back decades, the legend as we know it today gained significant traction in the late 1990s and early 2000s through online forums and personal accounts. These initial stories typically involved encounters with children who approached unsuspecting individuals, often late at night or in secluded areas, and made strange, sinister requests such as asking for a ride or entry into their homes. The chilling aspect of these encounters was not only the children's unsettling appearance but also the strange, inexplicable fear they instilled in their victims. The early accounts created an atmosphere of dread and mystery, attracting attention from individuals fascinated by the unexplained.

As time went on, the Black-Eyed Kids legend underwent multiple transformations and expanded its reach through various mediums. With the advent of social media, online communities dedicated to the paranormal flourished, providing a platform for people to share their personal encounters with these enigmatic beings. As more and more accounts were shared, patterns and recurring themes emerged, adding depth and complexity to the mythos surrounding the Black-Eyed Kids. This collective storytelling allowed the legend to evolve, with each new encounter contributing to the overall narrative arc.

The transformation of the Black-Eyed Kids legend also owes much to the influence of popular culture, particularly horror movies and literature. In recent years, horror movies featuring these eerie entities have gained significant traction, introducing a wider audience to the legend and further fueling its popularity. These on-screen representations often depict the Black-Eyed Kids as malicious beings, capable of inflicting fear and harm. As a result, the legend has taken on a darker and more malevolent tone, aligning with contemporary horror trends.

Furthermore, the proliferation of media channels, including YouTube channels, podcasts, and blogs, dedicated to exploring paranormal phenomena has become a significant catalyst in the evolution of the Black-Eyed Kids legend. These platforms offer a space for individuals to share their encounters, discuss theories, and engage with others who have similar interests. Additionally, the creators of this content often combine personal accounts with in-depth research and analysis, adding an academic layer to the discussion. This melding of personal narratives and scholarly exploration has resulted in a multifaceted approach to understanding and discussing the Black-Eyed Kids phenomenon, making it more accessible and appealing to a broader audience.

Alongside the influence of social media, popular culture, and paranormal research communities, the Black-Eyed Kids legend has also undergone a process of regional adaptation. Originating primarily in the United States, the legend now transcends borders and has found resonance in different parts of the world. Local variations and cultural adaptations have emerged, incorporating traditional folklore elements and unique societal fears related to children and the supernatural. These regional adaptations not only enrich the legend's narrative landscape but also serve to connect individuals across different cultures, creating a global community interested in sharing and exploring tales of the unknown. Through online communities, horror movies, and the proliferation of media channels dedicated to paranormal phenomena, the legend has gained momentum and taken on new dimensions. The collective storytelling and academic approaches to understanding these mysterious encounters have contributed to the legend's appeal, making it both approachable and friendly to those interested in the unknown. As the legend continues to evolve, it is likely that the Black-Eyed Kids will remain a captivating and terrifying presence in the realm of urban legends.

Chapter 9: The Haunted Clown Statue Legend

HISTORICAL BACKGROUND of the Haunted Clown Statue myth

Urban legends are timeless tales that blur the line between fact and fiction, often leading to chilling and terrifying narratives. The Haunted Clown Statue myth fits into this category, as it combines elements of horror and the supernatural. While the exact origins of this urban legend are uncertain, it is believed to have originated in the United States, where it quickly gained notoriety.

One possible explanation for the myth's origin lies in its ability to tap into people's innate fears. Coulrophobia, or the fear of clowns, is a well-documented psychological phenomenon that has long fascinated and haunted individuals. The Haunted Clown Statue myth likely harnesses this fear, using it as a potent tool to evoke a sense of dread and unease in those who hear the story. By incorporating a seemingly innocuous object like a clown statue into the narrative, the myth takes on an eerie quality that lingers long after it is first shared.

The story of the Haunted Clown Statue typically involves a protagonist or a group of characters who encounter a clown statue that seems to possess a malevolent presence. As the tale unfolds, the statue's behavior becomes increasingly sinister, leading to a climactic twist or reveal that leaves the characters and the audience shaken. This simple yet effective narrative structure has allowed the myth to spread rapidly through word of mouth, making it a staple of campfire stories and sleepover conversations.

The myth has evolved over time, with subtle variations appearing in different retellings. Some versions emphasize the statue's haunted origins, suggesting that it may be possessed by the spirit of a deceased clown or have ties to a tragic incident. Others add elements of psychological horror, with the statue seemingly moving or changing its expression when no one is looking. These adaptations serve to heighten the tension and intrigue surrounding the myth, ensuring its continued popularity.

The Haunted Clown Statue myth's lasting power can be attributed, in part, to its integration into popular culture. Numerous horror movies, books, and television shows have incorporated elements of this urban legend, further cementing its status as a cultural touchstone. These adaptations often introduce new variations, breathing new life into the myth and ensuring its ability to captivate audiences across different mediums.

In recent years, the Haunted Clown Statue myth has been further amplified by the advent of the internet and social media. Online forums and platforms have become breeding grounds for urban legends and ghost stories, allowing individuals to share their own experiences or interpretations of the myth. This digital landscape has facilitated the myth's proliferation, creating a virtual space where people can connect, discuss, and even construct their own narratives around the Haunted Clown Statue. Its emergence in the early 1980s coincides with the rise of contemporary horror culture, making it a prominent and enduring part of popular folklore. As the myth continues to evolve and find new manifestations within popular culture, its ability to captivate both storytellers and audiences alike underscores its timeless appeal. Whether one encounters the Haunted Clown Statue myth around a campfire, through a chilling movie, or online, it remains a testament to the power of storytelling and the enduring fascination with the eerie and macabre.

The psychological fear of clowns

To fully comprehend the fear of clowns, it is essential to explore its origins and historical context. The association between clowns and fear can be traced back to ancient times, where jesters and tricksters were considered both comic and menacing. However, the modern manifestation of coulrophobia can be attributed mainly to popular culture and media. The portrayal of clowns in horror films, novels, and television shows has ingrained a chilling image of these normally jovial characters in our collective consciousness. Coupled with the element of surprise that clowns often employ, the fear birthed by this combination is understandable. Therefore, it is crucial to acknowledge the role of media in instilling and perpetuating coulrophobia, as it significantly impacts individuals' perception of clowns.

Understanding the psychology behind coulrophobia offers valuable insights into why this specific fear is so potent. The fear of clowns can be categorized under the broader umbrella of specific phobias, which are characterized by an intense and irrational fear of a specific object or situation. This fear can cause considerable distress and interfere with a person's daily life. Numerous theories have been proposed to explain why coulrophobia develops, including the uncanny valley theory and the fear of the unknown. The uncanny valley theory posits that humans experience discomfort and fear when confronted with objects that resemble humans but are not quite realistic. Clowns, with their exaggerated features and eccentric behavior, often fall into this unsettling category. The fear of the unknown suggests that the ambiguity and unpredictability associated with clowns create anxiety, as individuals cannot fully anticipate their intentions or feelings. Exploring these psychological theories provides a framework for understanding the complexities of coulrophobia.

It is essential to acknowledge that coulrophobia is a genuine fear experienced by many individuals, and it should not be dismissed or ridiculed. Just as with any other phobia, it is crucial to approach those suffering from coulrophobia with empathy and understanding. Ridding oneself of this fear is not an instantaneous process but rather a journey that requires time, patience, and potentially professional assistance. Cognitive-behavioral therapy (CBT) has proven to be an effective treatment for specific phobias, including coulrophobia. CBT involves identifying and challenging irrational thoughts and beliefs related to clowns, gradually exposing oneself to clown-related stimuli in a controlled environment, and learning coping strategies to manage anxiety. This evidence-based approach grants individuals the tools necessary to confront their fear in a safe and structured manner, fostering a gradual desensitization.

However, it is worth mentioning that not everyone afflicted with coulrophobia may seek professional treatment. Therefore, self-help strategies can also be beneficial for individuals looking to alleviate their fear of clowns. These strategies involve gradual exposure to clown-related stimuli, beginning with less intimidating forms such as cartoons or pictures and gradually progressing towards more realistic representations. The use of relaxation techniques, such as deep breathing exercises or mindfulness meditation, can also aid in managing anxiety associated with clowns. The nurturing of a supportive environment and seeking reassurance from trusted individuals can further contribute to a sense of safety and comfort as individuals confront their fear. By examining its historical context, psychological foundations, and potential avenues for treatment, we can demystify this fear and alleviate its impact on individuals' lives. As we delve into the intriguing world of coulrophobia, it is crucial to maintain a friendly and approachable tone, fostering empathy and support for those who experience this fear. Together, we can unravel the mysteries surrounding the fear of clowns and empower individuals to conquer their fears, ultimately bringing about a more inclusive and clown-friendly society.

Modern adaptations of the Haunted Clown Statue legend in film and literature

In recent years, film has become a powerful vessel for conveying the terrifying nature of the Haunted Clown Statue legend. Directors and screenwriters have skillfully brought this chilling tale to life, utilizing the visual medium to instill fear and suspense in the hearts of audiences. Properties like Stephen King's "It," both the 1990 miniseries and its 2017 and 2019 film adaptations, have breathed new life into the Haunted Clown Statue legend. These adaptations effectively capture the essence of the legend, utilizing atmospheric cinematography, exceptional acting, and haunting musical scores. By exploring the depths of the human psyche, they tap into our deepest fears, perpetuating the chilling presence of the Haunted Clown Statue in our collective consciousness.

Literature, too, has embraced the Haunted Clown Statue legend, providing a platform for authors to explore the intricacies of fear and the supernatural. Writers have taken the core elements of the legend and expanded upon them, integrating complex characters and intricate plotlines that delve into the darkest corners of human nature. Works such as "The Clown Statue" by Fredric

Brown and "Scary Stories to Tell in the Dark" by Alvin Schwartz have disseminated the legend to a wide audience. These adaptations not only offer thrills and chills but also offer a deeper exploration of fear itself, examining its origins and effects on human psychology.

The impact of modern adaptations of the Haunted Clown Statue legend on popular culture cannot be overstated. These adaptations have not only influenced the horror genre but have also infiltrated mainstream media and consumer products. The image of a malevolent clown statue has become an icon, a symbol of fear that has permeated our society. In the age of social media, viral videos of clown sightings and creepy clown sightings have become a popular phenomenon, further perpetuating the legend's influence on popular culture. Additionally, costume parties and haunted attractions have embraced the eerie allure of the Haunted Clown Statue legend, capitalizing on the fear-inducing potential it holds for thrill-seekers worldwide.

One may wonder why the Haunted Clown Statue legend continues to captivate audiences and retain its relevance in modern adaptations. Perhaps it is the universal fear generated by the uncanny nature of clowns that strikes a chord within us. The juxtaposition of a clown, a traditionally jovial and entertaining figure, with a malevolent presence creates an unsettling tension that lies at the core of this legend's appeal. Moreover, the Haunted Clown Statue legend speaks to our primal fear of the unknown and the inability to trust our own senses. It taps into our deepest anxieties, exposing our vulnerability and reminding us that even the most innocent of objects can harbor a sinister secret. The visual medium of film and the written word have provided fertile ground for exploring the depths of fear and the supernatural. These adaptations have made an indelible impact on popular culture, perpetuating the legend's influence in various forms of media. The enduring power of the Haunted Clown Statue legend lies in its ability to evoke universal fears and exploit our vulnerabilities. As long as human beings continue to be fascinated by the dark recesses of the human psyche, this chilling legend will continue to captivate and haunt our collective imagination.

Chapter 10: The Cursed Phone Number

THE ORIGINS OF THE cursed phone number urban legend

It was during this time that rumors began to circulate about a specific phone number that carried a mysterious curse. According to the legend, dialing this number would lead to ominous consequences, with some even claiming that anyone who called it would meet a tragic end within a set amount of time. The specific details of the curse varied in each telling, but the underlying fear and intrigue surrounding this supposed cursed phone number remained consistent.

As the telephone network expanded and technology advanced, the legend evolved alongside it. In the decades that followed, people began to associate the cursed phone number with various terrifying experiences, such as receiving threatening or eerie messages, hearing unsettling voices on the line, or experiencing strange and unexplained occurrences after making the call. These stories spread through word-of-mouth, adding to the allure and fear factor of the legend.

The cursed phone number urban legend gained further traction and notoriety with the rise of internet culture. Online forums, chat rooms, and social media platforms became breeding grounds for sharing and discussing creepy stories, including accounts of encounters with the cursed number. This newfound digital space allowed the legend to reach a wider audience, both geographically and demographically, and contributed to its enduring popularity.

But where did this urban legend truly originate. It's challenging to pinpoint a specific event or person that gave birth to the cursed phone number myth.

Instead, this legend appears to have evolved organically through a combination of human fascination with the unknown, the allure of the mysterious, and our instinctive desire to share and spread captivating tales.

Similar to other urban legends, the cursed phone number legend likely draws on widespread fears and anxieties that exist in society. Communication technology has always carried an element of uncertainty and unease, from the fear of unwanted intrusions to the potential for miscommunication or manipulation. The cursed number urban legend taps into these anxieties, providing a tangible symbol for our collective unease about the mysteries and dangers that may lurk behind the seemingly innocuous world of telephony.

While the origins of the cursed phone number urban legend may remain shrouded in mystery, its enduring popularity and continued circulation are clear indicators of the human fascination with the macabre and the unexplained. Whether it's a cautionary tale, a form of entertainment, or simply a primal expression of our fear of the unknown, this legend serves as a reminder of how stories can take on a life of their own and capture our imagination across generations and mediums. While the exact origins of this legend may remain elusive, its enduring popularity and ability to spark fear and intrigue provide insight into our collective fascination with the unknown and our innate desire to share captivating stories. Whether it's a cautionary tale, a form of entertainment, or a manifestation of deeper societal fears, the cursed phone number urban legend continues to thrive in our modern, interconnected world.

The psychological effects of the cursed phone number myth

One of the most intriguing aspects of the cursed phone number myth is its ability to captivate and fascinate individuals. Humans are natural storytellers, and we thrive on narratives that challenge and engage our emotions. This urban legend taps into the depths of our psychological makeup, feeding our innate curiosity and fear of the unknown. The idea of a phone number that holds the power to bring about dire consequences sparks our imagination and encourages us to ponder the existence of supernatural forces. This curiosity, combined with the story's allure, can often lead individuals to seek out and investigate the alleged cursed number, further fueling their obsession and fixation.

When individuals come across the cursed phone number myth, they may initially dismiss it as mere fiction. However, as the narrative gains traction and is shared among peers, doubts begin to emerge. The power of suggestion plays a crucial role in shifting one's perspective from skepticism to belief. As individuals hear firsthand accounts or read the alleged experiences of those who claim to have encountered misfortune after calling the cursed number, their doubts start to waver. The fear of the unknown, coupled with personal anecdotes, can easily override rational thinking, leading individuals to attribute subsequent negative events in their lives to the supposed curse associated with the phone number.

The psychological impact of the cursed phone number myth goes beyond mere curiosity and belief. For some individuals, the constant fear and anxiety associated with it can be overwhelming and debilitating. A fear of making phone calls, particularly to unknown or potentially "cursed" numbers, can develop as a result. This fear, known as telephonophobia, may manifest as physical symptoms such as increased heart rate, sweating, or even panic attacks. The fear of cursing oneself or others by simply dialing a phone number can impose significant limitations on an individual's daily life, hindering their ability to communicate effectively or even seek help during emergencies.

Moreover, the cursed phone number myth can have a lasting impact on individuals' mental well-being. The constant worry of encountering misfortune or inadvertently causing harm to oneself or loved ones can lead to heightened levels of anxiety and stress. This chronic stress can have far-reaching consequences, including disrupted sleep patterns, decreased concentration levels, and impaired social functioning. Individuals may become increasingly isolated and withdrawn as they try to avoid situations that involve making phone calls or discussing the topic for fear of triggering anxiety or panic. The toll on mental health can be particularly challenging for those already prone to anxiety disorders or other psychological vulnerabilities.

It is important to note that the psychological effects of the cursed phone number myth may vary from person to person. While some individuals may remain unaffected and view it simply as an entertaining tale, others may be significantly impacted. Consequently, debunking such myths, providing accurate information, and promoting critical thinking are crucial steps in alleviating the unnecessary fear and anxiety associated with the cursed phone number myth. While it may be easy to dismiss such urban legends as mere superstition, their impact on individuals' mental well-being can be profound.

The power of suggestion, coupled with innate curiosity and fear of the unknown, can lead individuals to believe in the existence of supernatural forces associated with a particular phone number. This belief, in turn, may give rise to heightened anxiety, fear, and even phobia-like symptoms related to making phone calls or encountering unknown numbers. Recognizing the psychological implications of such myths and promoting critical thinking can go a long way in helping individuals navigate the complexities of their fears and maintain their mental well-being.

Real-life incidents related to the cursed phone number legend

One such fascinating urban legend that has persisted over the years is the notion of a cursed phone number. This chilling tale suggests that dialing a certain phone number can unleash a series of inexplicable and often horrifying events. While skeptics dismiss it as mere superstition, there have been several reported incidents that seem to lend credence to the legend. In this exploration, we will delve into some of these real-life incidents, examining their eerie nature and the impact they have had on the people involved. Prepare to enter the enigmatic realm of cursed phone numbers.

Incident 1: The Unsettling Suicide

One of the most well-known incidents related to the cursed phone number legend revolves around the tragic story of Tom. Tom, a curious and adventurous teenager, allegedly discovered the cursed phone number through an online forum. Tempted by the mystery, he decided to dial the number late one night, unaware of the grave consequences it would bring. The next morning, Tom was found dead in his room, having taken his own life. The circumstances surrounding his suicide were inexplicably disturbing, leaving authorities baffled and those close to him traumatized. This incident serves as a chilling reminder of the potential dangers associated with engaging with the cursed phone number.

Incident 2: The Unexplained Disappearance

Another unnerving occurrence linked to the cursed phone number reveals the story of Sara, a young woman seeking a thrill amid the mundanity of life. Intrigued by the rumors swirling around the mystical number, Sara, against her better judgment, resolved to call it. Immediately after dialing, Sara lost all contact with the world - her friends, family, and even her digital footprint vanished entirely. Despite exhaustive investigations by law enforcement agencies, no trace of Sara has ever been found. This mysterious disappearance has left many wondering if the cursed phone number holds the power to erase individuals from existence itself.

Incident 3: The Haunting Nightmares

In yet another spine-chilling case, a middle-aged man named John was plagued by a relentless series of harrowing nightmares following his encounter with the notorious phone number. As the legend suggests, dialing the cursed number brought forth a deluge of horrifying imagery, tormenting John's sleep and causing severe distress during his waking hours. Seeking refuge in therapy, John shared his experiences, which left even the most seasoned mental health professionals perplexed. The nightmares continued to haunt him relentlessly, leading some to believe there may be a sinister force at play, connecting dreams and the cursed phone number.

Incident 4: The Mysterious Illness

A particularly bizarre incident linked to the cursed phone number legend is that of Rebecca, a vibrant young woman who dialed the number out of morbid curiosity. Shortly after making the call, Rebecca began experiencing a range of unexplained ailments, ranging from inexplicable headaches to severe fatigue and even occasional bouts of amnesia. Countless medical consultations failed to provide a scientific explanation for her symptoms, leaving medical professionals astounded. For Rebecca and those close to her, the cursed phone number became intertwined with her physical well-being, reinforcing the unsettling notion that there is an untold power lurking behind this enigmatic legend.

WHILE SKEPTICS CONTINUE to dismiss the cursed phone number legend as nothing more than fiction, these real-life incidents cast a shadow of doubt on such dismissal. From suicide to mysterious disappearances, haunting nightmares to unexplained illnesses, these incidents have left a trail of fear and bewilderment in their wake. The phenomenon surrounding the cursed phone number remains shrouded in mystery, leaving us with more questions than answers. Whether one believes in the supernatural or not, these accounts serve as a chilling reminder of the unknown forces that may lurk just beyond our reach. Caution and curiosity must always coexist in our quest for understanding, lest we too become entangled in the web of the cursed phone number legend.

Chapter 11: The Legend of the Vanishing Hotel

THE HAUNTING TALES of disappearing hotels

One such eerie tale takes us to the heart of New Orleans, where the infamous Hotel Monteleone once stood. This elegant establishment, renowned for its Southern charm and hospitality, suddenly vanished from the bustling streets of the French Quarter. Locals share chilling accounts of a spectral presence that haunts the vacant lot where the hotel once stood. Some believe that the spirits of former guests, unwilling to depart, continue to wander the site, forever bound to the memories and experiences they forged within the hotel's walls. Others speculate that the hotel builders may have unwittingly disturbed an ancient burial ground, awakening vengeful spirits that now guard the lost hotel's secrets.

Moving across the Atlantic, we encounter the fascinating story of the Grand Hotel Polanki, perched on the rugged cliffs of Cornwall, England. This iconic hotel captivated visitors with its breathtaking views of the Atlantic Ocean. However, in an inexplicable turn of events, the hotel vanished overnight, leaving behind nothing but stunned witnesses and bewildered locals. Some theories suggest that an unprecedented geological event caused the entire building to be sucked into an underground cavern, forever hidden from human sight. Others whisper of otherworldly forces at play, asserting that the hotel was never meant to exist in our reality and was thus reclaimed by the forces that govern the supernatural realm.

Closer to home, the tale of the Vanishing Inn nestled amidst the remote forests of the Pacific Northwest sends shivers down the spines of those who encounter it. This isolated inn was known for its rustic charm and serene surroundings, drawing guests seeking solace and a break from the chaos of everyday life. But as stories go, the inn mysteriously vanished, leaving behind only a small clearing where it once stood. Locals speak of a ghostly figure appearing in the distance, occasionally glimpsed by brave hikers who dare to venture too close to the vanished inn. Theories abound, with some speculating that the inn strayed into a parallel dimension, where it continues to provide refuge for weary travelers who unknowingly stumble upon its hidden portal.

These stories of disappearing hotels not only ignite our imagination but also invite us to question the boundaries between the known and unknown, reality and the supernatural. While these tales may seem fantastical at first, they have inspired intense fascination among researchers, paranormal investigators, and skeptics alike.

Various theories have emerged over the years, attempting to provide rational explanations for these mysterious occurrences. Some point to natural phenomena, such as sinkholes or shifting tectonic plates, as potential culprits in the disappearance of these hotels. Others propose more exotic theories involving interdimensional travel or temporal rifts. However, the lack of concrete evidence and the sheer strangeness of these events continue to defy easy explanations.

In this book, we will delve into these theories, analyzing their merits and exploring their limitations. We will interview eyewitnesses, delve into historical records, and consult experts in the fields of geology, physics, and parapsychology to unravel the secrets of these disappearing hotels. By examining the haunting stories that surround them and approaching the subject with a balanced and open mindset, we hope to shed light on these perplexing enigmas and invite readers to form their own conclusions.

As we embark on this journey together, let us embrace the mysteries that lie within the world of disappearing hotels, and unleash our curiosity to unearth the truth that lies hidden within their vanished walls. Whether you are a skeptic or a believer, an adventurer or a lover of tales, this book promises to transport you to the heart of the extraordinary, inviting you to contemplate the unknown and challenge the boundaries of our understanding. So buckle up and prepare for a captivating adventure into the haunting tales of disappearing hotels.

Possible explanations for the Vanishing Hotel legend

Among these tales stands the enigmatic Vanishing Hotel legend, a story that has persisted through the ages. As with any legend, numerous theories and explanations have emerged attempting to shed light on the origins and potential truth behind this intriguing narrative. In this article, we aim to explore some of the most plausible explanations for the Vanishing Hotel legend, delving into historical events, psychological phenomena, and paranormal theories to offer a multifaceted analysis. Join us as we embark on a journey through the realm of mystery and speculation, seeking to unravel the secrets of this captivating legend.

Historical Perspective:

To understand the Vanishing Hotel legend, it is crucial to examine historical events that might have laid the foundation for its conception. Many believe that the legend finds its origins in the era of Prohibition, a period ranging from 1920 to 1933 when the sale, production, and distribution of alcoholic beverages were prohibited in the United States. During this time, hidden establishments known as speakeasies emerged to cater to the demand for illicit drinks. It is likely that the clandestine nature of these establishments, often hidden within seemingly ordinary buildings, contributed to the birth of the Vanishing Hotel legend. The illusion of a vanishing hotel may have been a cleverly devised façade to protect the secret activities of these speakeasies from law enforcement.

Psychological Explanations:

Beyond historical events, psychological phenomenon may also offer an explanation for the Vanishing Hotel legend. One potential theory centers around pareidolia, a psychological phenomenon in which individuals perceive significant patterns or meanings in random stimuli. According to this theory, the Vanishing Hotel legend might be a result of pareidolic interpretations of ordinary changes in the urban landscape. For instance, a hotel undergoing renovation or a building covered by scaffolding could give the impression of a disappearing establishment, leading to the formation of a tale that captures the imagination of the locals.

Paranormal Theories:

As with many legends, paranormal theories have also been woven into the tapestry of the Vanishing Hotel narrative. One prevalent belief is that these hotels exist on a supernatural plane, appearing to individuals at specific moments in time or dimensions. Some speculate that these ethereal establishments are portals to parallel universes or alternate dimensions, allowing glimpses into a reality that intertwines with our own. This theory often combines elements of time travel, interdimensional travel, and spiritual encounters, providing a spine-tingling explanation for the vanishing phenomenon.

The Role of Urban Legends:

Examining the Vanishing Hotel legend through the lens of urban legends offers another intriguing perspective. Urban legends are stories rooted in contemporary culture that embody shared fears, anxieties, and societal issues. They serve as cautionary tales or moral myths, often spread through word of mouth or via media platforms. The Vanishing Hotel legend could be seen as a cautionary tale about the transient nature of material possessions, the impermanence of the physical world, or a metaphor for the passage of time. This perspective allows us to explore the deeper meanings behind the legend and understand its cultural significance.

THE VANISHING HOTEL legend, with its captivating allure and mystical charm, has enthralled both skeptics and believers alike for generations. By examining the various explanations presented here, we have delved into the historical, psychological, and paranormal perspectives surrounding this intriguing tale. Whether rooted in the era of Prohibition, pareidolia-induced perceptions, interdimensional travel, or the realm of urban legends, these theories contribute to the rich tapestry of myths and folklore that captivate our collective imagination. While the truth may remain elusive, the legend continues to fascinate and inspire, inviting us to explore the realm of the unknown and embrace the magic that lies within our own narratives.

Urban legends related to haunted places and locations

One widely known urban legend revolves around the infamous haunted house on Elm Street. According to the legend, the house was the site of a gruesome murder in the early 1900s, and its ghostly inhabitants continue to haunt the premises to this day. Locals have reported hearing eerie sounds, witnessing flickering lights, and experiencing an unshakable feeling of being watched whenever they pass by the house. The tale has consistently captured the imaginations of thrill-seekers and paranormal enthusiasts alike, drawing them to witness the alleged haunting firsthand.

The allure of haunted places like the house on Elm Street lies not only in the supernatural elements but also in the communal experience they generate. Urban legends allow communities to create a shared narrative, reinforcing group cohesion and identity. Tales of haunted locations can become an integral part of a community's folklore, passed from one generation to the next as a way to preserve the area's rich history. Whether or not the alleged haunting is based in reality, the stories surrounding these places serve as a form of cultural heritage, connecting individuals to their past and creating a sense of belonging.

It is important, however, to approach these legends with a critical eye. Often, real historical events become distorted over time, blending truth and fiction until the line between the two becomes blurred. The paranormal elements of these tales can be traced back to the very human tendency to seek meaning and explanations for the unknown. We attribute supernatural activity to unexplainable phenomena, providing comfort in an otherwise chaotic world. By exploring the psychological underpinnings of urban legends related to haunted places, we can better understand why they persist in contemporary society.

Another haunting urban legend that has captured the public's fascination is that of St. Agnes Hospital, a dilapidated institution shrouded in eerie stories. Legend has it that St. Agnes Hospital was a place of unspeakable horrors, where patients were subjected to grotesque experiments, and their tormented souls now inhabit the crumbling halls. Urban explorers and ghost hunters flock to the decaying structure in search of chilling encounters that will validate the haunting rumors. The legend does not discriminate, captivating both the skeptical and the believers, as they venture into the dark unknown.

Haunted places often become popular destinations for thrill-seekers, paranormal investigators, and curious visitors hoping to catch a glimpse of the supernatural. The allure of the unknown draws in individuals from various walks of life, providing a platform for shared experiences and discussions. In this sense, urban legends related to haunted locations serve as a catalyst for social interaction and the formation of new connections. Whether participants believe in the paranormal or not, the shared excitement surrounding these legends has the power to bring people together.

While the tales of haunted places continue to fascinate and entertain us, it is essential to approach them with a healthy dose of skepticism. The human mind is adept at conjuring elaborate stories, especially when fueled by a combination of fear, anticipation, and a desire for thrill. As we delve into the narratives surrounding haunted places, this book urges readers to critically analyze the sources, evaluate the evidence, and question the veracity of the stories. By doing so, we can separate fact from fiction, gaining a deeper understanding of the psychology behind these urban legends. These stories not only provide a source of entertainment but also serve as a means of preserving cultural history and fostering community cohesion. However, it is crucial to approach these legends with a critical mindset, understanding the psychological mechanisms that perpetuate their existence. By examining the origins and dynamics of these urban legends, we can unravel the mysteries they hold and gain insight into the human fascination with the unknown.

Chapter 12: The La Llorona Curse

THE LEGEND OF LA LLORONA in Latin American folklore

The story of La Llorona is deeply rooted in Latin American history and has various iterations depending on the region. However, its central narrative typically revolves around a beautiful woman who is betrayed by her husband or lover. In some versions, La Llorona is a young indigenous woman who falls in love with a Spanish conquistador. Despite their differences in social status, the couple has two children together. However, the conquistador eventually abandons La Llorona to marry a woman of his own class, leaving her heartbroken and desperate.

Unable to bear the pain of her abandonment, La Llorona drowns her children in a river out of anger and despair. Soon after realizing the horrific act she has committed, she is overcome with remorse and drowns herself as well. It is said that her anguished spirit roams the earth, forever searching for her lost children, causing her to be known as "The Weeping Woman." Some variations of the legend add that La Llorona seeks out other children, mistaking them for her own, and brings them to a watery grave.

The legend of La Llorona serves as a cautionary tale, warning against the destructive consequences of selfishness, betrayal, and the overwhelming power of grief. However, it also speaks to deeper cultural anxieties and fears related to issues of identity, societal hierarchies, and colonization. The character of La Llorona embodies the complexities of womanhood, the hardships faced by marginalized communities, and the enduring traumas of conquest and loss.

While the story of La Llorona is undeniably eerie and haunting, it also offers an opportunity for reflection and understanding. The theme of maternal love and the lengths a mother would go to protect her children resonates deeply with audiences across cultures. The story elicits empathy and compassion, allowing us to explore our own emotions and contemplate the consequences of our actions.

Furthermore, the legend of La Llorona has also become a significant part of popular culture, making its way into literature, film, and art. Many authors and filmmakers have reimagined the tale, offering their interpretations and bringing the legend to a broader audience. These adaptations contribute to the continued relevance of La Llorona, keeping her story alive and allowing new generations to engage with this rich folklore.

It is worth noting that the legend of La Llorona is not confined to the realm of fiction. Many people claim to have had personal encounters with her spirit, reporting ethereal weeping sounds and sightings of a ghostly figure wandering near bodies of water. These accounts have further added to the mystique and allure surrounding the legend, blurring the lines between folklore and reality. It serves as a cautionary tale, exploring themes of love, betrayal, and the consequences of one's actions. The story of a grieving mother searching desperately for her lost children resonates deeply with audiences, inviting us to reflect on our own emotions and choices. The haunting nature of the legend has ensured its endurance over generations, further fueled by its presence in popular culture and reported encounters with La Llorona's spirit. Ultimately, La Llorona represents a potent and captivating figure in Latin American folklore, one that continues to intrigue and linger in our collective imagination.

Similar myths and legends from around the world

One of the most prevalent motifs in myths and legends across different cultures is the creation myth. Almost every civilization has its own version of how the world came into existence, often involving gods or supernatural beings. For example, the creation story of the ancient Sumerians tells of the god Enki and his battle against the chaotic forces of the sea to create order and establish civilization. Similarly, the Norse creation myth depicts the great giant Ymir, whose dismembered body forms the various elements of the natural world. Despite such differences, these creation myths share a common thread of a divine or primordial force bringing order and life to the world.

Another recurring theme in myths and legends from around the world is the hero's journey. This archetype can be traced back to the epic of Gilgamesh in Mesopotamia and finds its way into the Greek myths, the Hindu epics, and the Arthurian legends, among others. The hero's journey typically involves a protagonist who embarks on a perilous quest or adventure, facing dangerous challenges and overcoming them through bravery or cunning. This theme resonates with audiences as it reflects the universal human experience of grappling with adversity and the quest for self-discovery.

Furthermore, many cultures have their own version of a flood myth, where a cataclysmic deluge wipes out humanity, sparing only a select few who escape on a boat or some other form of vessel. The most famous flood myth comes from the biblical story of Noah's Ark, but similar tales exist in the ancient Indian texts, such as the story of Manu in the Rigveda, and in the mythology of the Native American tribes. These flood myths often convey a moral message about the consequences of human transgressions or the need for repentance, and they offer a cautionary tale to future generations about the dangers of moral corruption.

The concept of a trickster figure is another common thread that runs through myths and legends worldwide. Trickster figures, often represented as mischievous animals or deities, are known for their cunning and their ability to bend or defy the rules of the natural and social order. For example, the Norse trickster god Loki and the Native American figure Coyote both exhibit trickster characteristics and are known for their role in disrupting or challenging the established order. These trickster figures serve to remind humanity of the fragility of societal norms and the need for adaptability and humor in the face of adversity.

In addition to these themes, myths and legends often incorporate supernatural beings and fantastical creatures that are strikingly similar across different cultures. Dragons, for instance, appear in the mythology of Europe, Asia, and the Americas, albeit with some variations in their characteristics and symbolism. Similarly, the concept of the vampire exists in various forms in folklore from Eastern Europe, Asia, and Africa. These similarities in mythical creatures suggest a shared human fascination with the supernatural and the possibility of otherworldly realms.

While these examples provide a glimpse into the interconnectedness of myths and legends, it is important to note that cultural context and regional variations also play a significant role in shaping these narratives. Stories are deeply embedded in the cultural fabric of a society and serve as a reflection of its values, beliefs, and historical experiences. Therefore, even though similar themes and motifs may appear in myths and legends from around the world, the specific details and interpretations can differ significantly, showcasing the richness and diversity of human imagination and storytelling. Whether it is the creation myth, the hero's journey, the flood myth, the trickster figure, or the presence of supernatural creatures, these shared narrative elements transcend cultural boundaries and time periods. By exploring and comparing these myths and legends, we gain valuable insights into the collective human experience and the universal yearning for understanding and meaning. The study of similar myths and legends is not only a fascinating field of research but also a testament to the shared heritage of humanity, emphasizing our interconnectedness and the common threads that bind us together as a species.

The symbolism and themes of the La Llorona curse

At its core, the curse of La Llorona symbolizes the consequences of neglecting one's responsibilities and failing to prioritize loved ones. The story revolves around a woman who, consumed by her own desires and female rage, neglects and ultimately kills her own children. This act of maternal betrayal and abandonment exposes the dark side of motherhood, highlighting the intense pressure and societal expectations placed on women to fulfill their maternal duties flawlessly. Furthermore, La Llorona represents the archetype of the grieving mother, mourning the loss of her children, which touches upon the universal theme of loss and the harrowing pain associated with it.

Underneath the symbolism lies another important theme present in the La Llorona curse – the role of women in Mexican culture and society. La Llorona serves as a cautionary tale for women, reminding them of the consequences that may befall them if they deviate from societal norms or defy societal expectations. By emphasizing the themes of neglected motherhood and female rage, the legend reinforces the prevailing patriarchal framework that expects women to conform to prescribed gender roles. It serves as a reminder of the dire consequences that women may face when they challenge the status quo or assert their own agency.

The symbolism of water in the story of La Llorona further enriches its themes and impacts. Water represents cleansing, purification, and rebirth – all of which are encompassed within the narrative. La Llorona's haunting wails and searches for her children often occur near bodies of water, such as rivers or lakes. This association with water underscores the idea of emotional cleansing and the need for individuals, in particular women, to confront and release their deep-seated emotions and trauma. It acts as a reminder of the importance of addressing one's emotional wounds rather than letting them fester and potentially harm oneself and others.

Moreover, the story of La Llorona can be seen as an allegory for the historical and ongoing mistreatment of Mexican women. It reflects the systemic violence, gender inequality, and societal injustices that women have endured throughout Mexican history. By embodying the experiences of countless women who have been silenced, oppressed, and denied justice, La Llorona represents the collective voice of women demanding recognition, empowerment, and equality.

Despite the haunting and dark nature of the La Llorona curse, the legend also offers a glimmer of hope and redemption. It emphasizes the importance of reflection, repentance, and forgiveness. In some variations of the story, La Llorona is depicted as a tormented soul who is forever trapped between the mortal and spirit worlds. This suggests that redemption and peace can only be achieved through the acknowledgement of one's wrongdoings and the genuine desire to make amends. It serves as a reminder that even in the face of despair, there is always the possibility of transformation and reconciliation. It addresses the themes of neglected motherhood, female rage, gender roles, and the mistreatment of women. The symbolism of water further enhances these themes, emphasizing the importance of emotional cleansing and confronting one's trauma. Ultimately, the story of La Llorona serves as a cautionary tale, reminding individuals of the consequences of neglecting their responsibilities and the potential for redemption and transformation.

Chapter 13: The Haunted Ouija Board

THE HISTORY AND ORIGINS of the Ouija board

The concept of talking boards and spirit communication can be traced back to ancient times. In ancient China, a practice known as "fuji" involved using a planchette to receive messages from the spirit world. Similar practices were also observed in Greece and Rome, where individuals sought to communicate with the deceased through various means.

The modern Ouija board as we know it today, however, originated in the late 19th century. In 1890, a group of entrepreneurs named Elijah Bond, Charles Kennard, and William Maupin teamed up with a novelty manufacturer named Isaac Fuld to create the first commercially available talking board. They filed for a patent, and in 1891, the Ouija board was born.

The etymology of the name "Ouija" itself has an intriguing history. According to popular belief, the name emerged during one of the board's early séances. Allegedly, when asked what the board should be called, the planchette spelled out "O-U-I-J-A." When questioned about the meaning, the board responded with "Good luck." This interpretation stuck, and the name Ouija board has prevailed ever since.

In the early days, the Ouija board was marketed as a harmless parlor game, intended to provide entertainment at social gatherings. However, it quickly gained a reputation for being a tool for spirit communication, attracting the attention of spiritualists and theosophists who believed in the reality of such connections.

One pivotal moment in the history of the Ouija board came in 1913 when William Fuld, who had since taken ownership of the board, died in a tragic accident. Fuld's death sparked rumors and superstitions that the Ouija board was cursed or possessed. These rumors elevated the board's mystique and contributed to its enduring popularity.

Over the years, the Ouija board has faced significant scrutiny from skeptics and critics. Many argue that the perceived messages are simply the result of subconscious movements by the participants, known as the ideomotor effect. This theory posits that when individuals place their hands on the planchette, slight involuntary movements create the appearance of directed motion.

Despite the skepticism and controversies surrounding the Ouija board, its popularity continued to grow throughout the 20th century. It featured prominently in popular culture, particularly in movies, books, and even songs. Its iconic design, with a board divided into letters, numbers, and symbols, has become instantly recognizable.

The Ouija board's continued popularity can be attributed to multiple factors. For some, it represents a sense of mystery and curiosity about the afterlife and the possibility of communication with spirits. Others view it as a form of entertainment and a way to connect with friends and family. Additionally, the Ouija board has been embraced by various spiritual and esoteric communities, who see it as a tool for divination and exploring the spiritual realm.

In recent years, the Ouija board has experienced a resurgence in popularity, thanks in part to the rise of paranormal investigation shows and the increasing interest in all things supernatural. However, it is important to note that the board itself does not possess any inherent power or ability to communicate with spirits. Its use is entirely reliant on the beliefs and intentions of those participating. Its modern incarnation was invented in the late 19th century and quickly gained popularity as a parlor game and a tool for spiritual exploration. Despite skepticism and controversy, the Ouija board continues to captivate, intrigue, and provide a platform for individuals to connect with the unknown. Whether one believes in its supernatural properties or not, the Ouija board remains an enduring symbol of curiosity about the afterlife and our longing to reach out to realms beyond our own.

The supernatural dangers associated with using a Ouija board

From ancient folklore to modern-day horror tales, our fascination with the paranormal continues to captivate us. In recent years, the usage of Ouija boards has gained popularity as a means to communicate with the supernatural realm. However, beneath their mystique, Ouija boards carry a potential for supernatural dangers that should not be taken lightly. In this comprehensive analysis, we will delve into the dark side of Ouija boards, exploring the potential hazards associated with their use.

1. The Ouija Board: A Gateway to the Unknown:

Ouija boards have a rich and mysterious history, dating back to the late 19th century when spiritualists introduced them as a tool for communication with the spirit world. This "talking board" consists of letters, numbers, and other symbols which users employ to receive messages from beyond. Although masquerading as a harmless game, the Ouija board can open a door to the supernatural, exposing users to a plethora of potential dangers.

2. The Psychological Effects:

One of the primary dangers associated with using a Ouija board lies within the psychological impact it can have on individuals. The experience itself can be overwhelmingly intense, sometimes leading to psychological distress, anxiety, and emotional upheaval. The unpredictable nature of the Ouija board's responses can create a sense of vulnerability, causing users to question their own sanity and fostering a state of paranoia.

Furthermore, the subconscious mind's susceptibility to suggestion can potentially lead individuals to believe in the authenticity of the messages received through the Ouija board, blurring the lines between reality and the supernatural. This amplifies the risk of adopting harmful beliefs, which may have long-lasting effects on one's mental well-being.

3. Spirits and Negative Entities:

The primary allure of a Ouija board lies in its ability to summon spirits and communicate with entities from the other side. However, not all spirits are benign, and by opening the door to communications, we may inadvertently invite negative entities into our lives. These malevolent spirits can pose a significant threat to an individual's psychological and emotional stability as they may seek to manipulate, torment, or possess unsuspecting participants.

Dangerous and malevolent entities can lurk within the spirit realm, and users of the Ouija board run the risk of attracting their attention. Inexperienced users, often thrill-seekers or those who approach the board with disrespectful intentions, are particularly vulnerable to the influence of these supernatural predators.

4. Hauntings and Attachments:

Another real danger associated with Ouija board usage is the potential for hauntings and attachments. Spirits who are channeled through the board may become attracted to the energy of the participants or the physical location where the board is used. This can lead to paranormal activities such as strange sounds, objects moving, and even physical attacks. Such experiences can cause severe distress and disruption in an individual's life, leading to physical harm, sleep disturbances, and an overall sense of foreboding.

Attachments occur when spirits, often those with negative intent, make a connection with an individual, latching onto their aura or energy field. This attachment can cause emotional and physical drain, leading to prolonged negative effects on the individual's overall well-being.

5. Manipulation and Deception:

The realm of the supernatural can be a deceptive one. When using a Ouija board, users open themselves up to potential manipulation, as deceptive spirits may masquerade as loved ones or friendly entities to gain trust and manipulate the situation to their advantage. This manipulation can lead individuals astray, causing them to make misguided decisions or engage in harmful practices under the influence of these entities.

WHILE THE SUPERNATURAL realm undeniably holds an allure, it is crucial to approach Ouija boards with caution and respect. The potential dangers associated with their use should not be dismissed, as they can have lasting impacts on an individual's mental, emotional, and even physical well-being. Understanding the psychological and supernatural risks is crucial before attempting to engage with the Ouija board. Remember, sometimes it is better to leave the mysteries of the supernatural unexplored, as the price of curiosity may be too steep to pay.

True stories of haunted Ouija board experiences

In this book, we will embark on a captivating journey of exploration and discovery, delving into the chilling true stories that have left people bewildered, fascinated, and maybe even terrified. If you've ever been captivated by the supernatural or have a burning curiosity about Ouija boards, this collection of experiences will quench your thirst for the paranormal. Join us as we unravel the stories behind haunted Ouija boards and shed light on the unexplained phenomena that have left their mark on countless individuals.

The Origins and Myths Surrounding Ouija Boards

To better understand the haunted Ouija board experiences we explore later, it is essential to familiarize ourselves with the origins and myths that surround Ouija boards. We will discuss the history of spirit communication devices, the creation of the Ouija board itself, and the various beliefs among different cultural and religious groups. Tackling lingering misconceptions, we will explore the science and psychology behind the board and its use, maintaining a balanced approach to the topic.

Spirits Unleashed - Opening the Gateway

In this one, we delve into the riveting stories of individuals who embarked on journeys by opening the gateway to another world using Ouija boards. These tales recount the excitement and trepidation of those who summoned spirits, inadvertently unleashing forces they may not have been prepared for. Lured by the promise of supernatural contact, these encounters range from the benign to the spine-tinglingly malevolent. We will examine the importance of precautions, respect, and understanding of the ritualistic aspects surrounding Ouija board sessions.

Encounters with the Unknown - Paranormal Manifestations

Venturing further into the heart of haunted Ouija board experiences, we explore the encounters that defy rational explanation. These stories delve into the eerie manifestations witnessed by the brave souls who dared to toy with the Ouija board. Readers will hear firsthand accounts of objects inexplicably moving, unexplained noises and whispers, chilling apparitions, and even physical interactions with unseen spirits. Through detailed analysis, we aim to shed light on the curious connection between the Ouija board and these haunting phenomena.

Malevolent Entities - Confronting Negative Experiences

Wrapped in darkness, this one explores the encounters with malevolent entities that emerged from the depths of Ouija board experiences. These terrifying moments reveal the dangers inherent when navigating the spiritual realm without caution or knowledge. While the stories may cause goosebumps, we will endeavor to provide insights on how to handle negative spirits, shield oneself from potential harm, and offer guidance for those seeking resolution or solace after distressing encounters.

Psychic Connections - Communication Beyond the Veil

Shedding light on a different facet of haunted Ouija board experiences, this one focuses on the instances where Ouija board sessions unveiled surprising psychic abilities within individuals. We will discuss extraordinary stories of heightened intuition, precognition, mediumship, and psychic visions that emerged during Ouija board sessions. These fascinating tales will challenge conventional beliefs and encourage deeper exploration of the untapped potential within our consciousness.

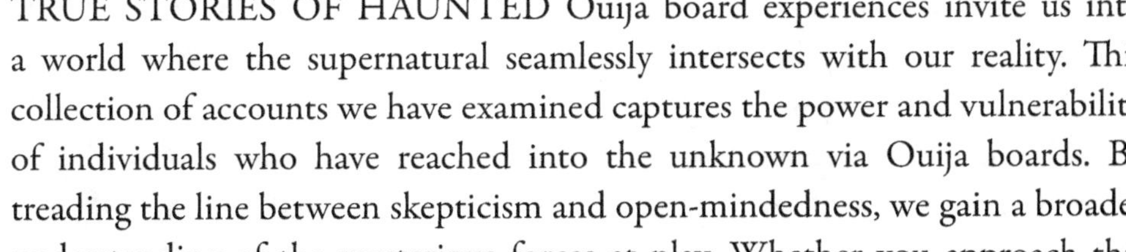

TRUE STORIES OF HAUNTED Ouija board experiences invite us into a world where the supernatural seamlessly intersects with our reality. This collection of accounts we have examined captures the power and vulnerability of individuals who have reached into the unknown via Ouija boards. By treading the line between skepticism and open-mindedness, we gain a broader understanding of the mysterious forces at play. Whether you approach this book as a skeptic, a believer, or a curious explorer, we hope it ignites a sense of wonder and encourages further inquiry into the world of the paranormal.

Chapter 14: The Killer in the Backseat Story

THE EVOLUTION OF THE Killer in the Backseat urban legend

One of the most enduring and chilling legends is that of the "Killer in the Backseat." This iconic tale has evolved over the years, captivating generations with its suspenseful narrative and thought-provoking message. In this one, we will explore the fascinating evolution of the Killer in the Backseat urban legend, tracing its origins, examining its variations across different cultures, and analyzing the enduring appeal of this spine-tingling tale.

Origins of the Legend:

Like many urban legends, the exact origins and specific details of the Killer in the Backseat tale remain elusive. However, it is believed to have emerged in the mid-20th century in America. Its earliest iterations typically featured a female protagonist driving alone late at night, when she becomes aware of a suspicious vehicle following her. Panicked, she speeds away, only to find a stranger hiding in her backseat, intending to harm her. The story often concludes with a twist: a helpful passerby alerts the protagonist to the danger, allowing her to escape unscathed.

Variations across Cultures:

As the Killer in the Backseat urban legend spread, it underwent cultural permutations, reflecting the fears and concerns of different societies. In Japan, for instance, the legend takes on a supernatural twist, with the attacker transforming into a ghost or a vengeful spirit. In Latin American countries, the legend often portrays the attacker as a deranged criminal or a member of a violent gang. Additionally, different settings, such as rural areas or crowded cities, have been incorporated into the narrative, providing new layers of suspense and relatability for diverse audiences worldwide.

Psychological Underpinnings:

The timeless and universal appeal of the Killer in the Backseat legend can be attributed to its exploitation of deep-seated human fears and anxieties. This collective dread of the unknown, vulnerability, and betrayal taps into our primal instincts for self-preservation. The fear of being stalked, trapped, or harmed by an unseen assailant resonates deeply, triggering a surge of adrenaline and an increased awareness of our surroundings. It is this visceral and captivating response that has allowed the legend to transcend cultural and generational boundaries.

Social and Technological Context:

As society has evolved, so too has the Killer in the Backseat urban legend. Advances in technology and communication have allowed for new variations of the legend to emerge. With the rise of rideshare platforms, for example, the tale has taken on a modern twist centered around strangers posing as drivers to commit heinous acts. The ubiquity of mobile phones has also shaped the narrative, introducing the potential for protagonist to call for help at crucial moments. These contemporary adaptations demonstrate how urban legends are not fixed in time but continue to evolve alongside our changing world.

Moral Lessons and Cultural Commentary:

Beyond its ability to frighten and captivate, the Killer in the Backseat legend serves as a cautionary tale, underscoring the importance of vigilance, self-awareness, and trust in society. By presenting scenarios in which ordinary individuals find themselves thrust into life-threatening situations, the legend encourages readers and listeners to remain cautious and mindful of their surroundings. Furthermore, the cultural and societal anxieties woven into the legend can shed light on deeper issues prevalent within a given context, such as the fear of strangers, crime rates, gender dynamics, and social norms.

THE EVOLUTION OF THE Killer in the Backseat urban legend reveals the power of storytelling to captivate and captivate audiences across different cultures and time periods. As this chilling tale has passed from one generation to another, it has shape-shifted to cater to the fears and concerns of each era. We are reminded of the enduring fascination humanity has with tales that both entertain and serve as cautionary reminders. In examining this legend, we acknowledge its ability to tap into our collective unconscious and inspire a renewed sense of vigilance in an unpredictable world.

Similar stories in popular culture and literature

To begin, let us explore the concept of archetypes, which are recurring character types, motifs, or plot structures found in storytelling across various cultures and eras. From the hero's journey to the forbidden love, archetypal stories fill the pages of literature and permeate popular culture in movies, television shows, and even advertising campaigns. By recognizing these archetypes, we can uncover the underlying patterns that make these narratives resonate with audiences from different backgrounds. The hero's journey, for example, presents a universal tale of a protagonist facing trials, discovering inner strength, and ultimately achieving victory. This archetype can be found in ancient epic poems like "The Odyssey" as well as in contemporary blockbusters such as "Star Wars." Understanding archetypes allows us to appreciate the connections between seemingly distinct stories and recognize the timeless themes that permeate our cultural experiences.

Another aspect of the similarities we find in popular culture and literature is the exploration of fundamental human emotions and experiences. These stories serve as mirrors reflecting our own desires, fears, and aspirations back to us. They provide a safe space for us to process and make sense of our own complex emotions. For instance, the theme of unrequited love has been explored in countless stories, from William Shakespeare's "Romeo and Juliet" to modern films such as "500 Days of Summer." Through these narratives, we are able to explore the complexities of emotions such as longing, heartbreak, and the search for connection. By recognizing these shared emotional experiences, we can foster empathy and understanding, transcending cultural and societal barriers.

Furthermore, similar stories in popular culture and literature often serve as vehicles for social commentary and critique. These narratives reflect the concerns and issues of their time, providing a platform to challenge societal norms or shed light on marginalized voices. For example, dystopian novels like George Orwell's "1984" or Margaret Atwood's "The Handmaid's Tale" portray nightmarish societies that serve as cautionary tales, warning us of the dangers of totalitarianism or the erosion of individual freedoms. Similarly, popular culture showcases stories that address contemporary issues such as racism, gender inequality, or socioeconomic disparities. By exploring these narratives, we are prompted to critically analyze our own society and question the power structures and ideologies that shape our world.

In addition to exploring archetypes, universal emotions, and societal critique, we must also acknowledge the role of intertextuality in creating similar stories in popular culture and literature. Intertextuality refers to the references, allusions, or adaptations that exist between different works of art. These connections often add depth and richness to narratives, creating a network of stories that build upon one another. For example, a movie may pay homage to a classic novel, or a television series may reference a famous film. By recognizing and understanding these intertextual references, we can gain deeper insights into the themes and ideas being explored, as well as the cultural context in which they originated. Intertextuality not only enriches our enjoyment of these stories but also encourages us to engage in a dialogue across different art forms and mediums.

Ultimately, the existence of similar stories in popular culture and literature reveals the universal nature of storytelling. Despite our diverse backgrounds and experiences, we all share a fundamental human need for narrative, connection, and understanding. These stories provide us with a common language that transcends cultural and generational boundaries. They allow us to explore our own identities and values while also fostering empathy and appreciation for perspectives different from our own. By recognizing the patterns and themes that permeate these narratives, we can deepen our understanding of ourselves and the world around us. In this book, we will embark on a journey to explore the rich tapestry of similar stories in popular culture and literature, unveiling the profound impact they have on our lives and the collective human experience.

The psychological fear of being followed or stalked

Being followed or stalked may evoke intense emotions of fear, helplessness, and anxiety. Individuals who experience this psychological fear often report feeling constantly watched or monitored, which can lead to a heightened state of hyper-vigilance. This heightened state of awareness and unease can affect many aspects of a person's life, such as personal relationships, professional pursuits, and overall well-being. It can be an isolating experience, as individuals may struggle to communicate their fears to others out of concern that they might not be taken seriously or that their concerns may be dismissed.

One common aspect of the psychological fear of being followed or stalked is the lack of control over personal space and privacy. Individuals who are being followed or stalked may experience intrusive thoughts and constantly feel that their personal boundaries are being violated. This can lead to a sense of powerlessness and vulnerability, as the person being followed may be unsure of the stalker's intentions or the extent of their knowledge about their private life. This constant fear can impact their ability to relax, trust others, or engage in activities they once enjoyed.

It is essential to recognize that the psychological fear of being followed or stalked is not a rational fear. While it is crucial for individuals to prioritize their safety and exercise caution in potentially dangerous situations, excessive fear and paranoia can negatively impact mental health and quality of life. Seeking professional help such as therapy or counseling can provide individuals with the necessary support and guidance to cope with and overcome their fear.

In addressing this fear, it is crucial to develop coping strategies that empower individuals and empower them to regain control over their lives. Establishing a support network of trusted friends, family, or professionals who can offer emotional support and practical guidance is an important step towards alleviating the psychological fear. Sharing experiences and concerns with others who have gone through similar experiences can also provide comfort and reassurance that one is not alone in their struggle.

Additionally, learning self-defense techniques or enrolling in a personal safety course can be empowering for individuals facing the psychological fear of being followed or stalked. Acquiring the necessary skills and knowledge to defend oneself can restore a sense of confidence and empower individuals to take action if they ever find themselves in a threatening situation. These measures not only enhance personal safety but can also serve as a deterrent to potential stalkers, as they may recognize that their intended victim is not an easy target.

Another important aspect to address is the role of law enforcement and legal measures in combating stalking and ensuring the safety of individuals. Reporting incidents promptly to the authorities is crucial, as it can help establish a legal record of the stalking behavior and provide necessary evidence for potential legal action. Victims should be familiar with the local laws pertaining to stalking and obtain appropriate advice on protective orders or restraining orders to ensure their safety.

Lastly, self-care and self-compassion are vital in overcoming the psychological fear of being followed or stalked. Engaging in activities that promote relaxation and stress reduction, such as meditation, yoga, or hobbies, can help individuals regain a sense of normalcy and provide a much-needed respite from the fear and anxiety that accompanies stalking. Taking care of one's physical health, such as getting regular exercise, maintaining a balanced diet, and getting sufficient sleep, is crucial for overall well-being and resilience in the face of adversity. It is a fear rooted in the perceived threat to personal safety, often leading to anxiety, paranoia, and a loss of control. By seeking support, developing coping strategies, understanding legal measures, and prioritizing self-care, individuals can reclaim their lives and work towards overcoming this fear. It is crucial to approach this topic with empathy, understanding, and awareness, as addressing the psychological fear of being followed or stalked requires a multifaceted and holistic approach to support and empower victims.

Chapter 15: The Haunted Doll Curse

THE HISTORY OF HAUNTED dolls and their origins

One of the earliest recorded instances of haunted dolls can be found in ancient Egypt. In this civilization, the concept of an inanimate object being imbued with a spirit or soul was not uncommon. Dolls were often used as symbolic representations of deities, including deities associated with death and the afterlife. These dolls were believed to carry the power and essence of these deities and were used in religious rituals and ceremonies.

Moving forward in time, in the Middle Ages, dolls took on a different role in society. They began to be used as protection against evil spirits and witches. Parents would often create "poppets" or small dolls made of cloth or clay to shield their children from harm. These poppets were thought to act as a surrogate for the child, absorbing any curses or malevolent energies directed towards them. However, over time, these protective dolls also became associated with darker and more sinister purposes.

As societies evolved and progressed, so too did the stories surrounding haunted dolls. In the 19th century, during the height of the Spiritualist movement, interest in the supernatural and the occult reached its peak. This era saw the rise of mediumship, séances, and the widespread belief in communicating with the deceased. Alongside this, haunted dolls began to gain more attention and popularity.

One of the most famous examples of a haunted doll from this period is the infamous Annabelle. The story of Annabelle originated in the 1970s when a nursing student received a Raggedy Ann doll as a gift and soon began experiencing strange and unsettling occurrences. The doll seemed to move on its own, leaving handwritten notes, and even attacking people. The story of Annabelle gained further notoriety when it was portrayed in several horror movies, perpetuating its status as a feared and haunted doll.

While some haunted dolls have gained celebrity status in popular culture, many others remain tucked away in attics or hidden in the recesses of museum archives. These lesser-known dolls have their own unique stories and origins, often surrounded by supernatural phenomena that defy rational explanation. Curators of haunted doll exhibits and collectors of these eerie objects often report peculiar happenings, such as unexplained whispers, moving objects, or a persistent feeling of being watched.

Exploring the origins of haunted dolls is not just an exercise in examining historical and cultural beliefs; it also delves into the human psyche. The concept of a haunted doll taps into our innate fear of the unknown, the uncanny, and the supernatural. Psychologically, dolls have the potential to evoke both positive and negative emotional responses. They can be seen as companions, symbols of innocence and playfulness, but they can also represent the boundary between the animate and inanimate, blurring the line between the living and the lifeless.

The haunting of dolls, whether real or perceived, can be attributed to a variety of factors. In some cases, personal experiences and trauma may provide a foundation for haunting narratives. Stories emerge from individuals projecting their fears and anxieties onto the inanimate object, creating a sense of malevolence and supernatural occurrences. External influences, such as legends, urban myths, and media portrayals, also shape the perception of haunted dolls and fuel their mystique.

In the present day, haunted dolls continue to captivate our collective imagination. With the rise of the internet and social media, these eerie stories and chilling photographs can be instantly shared and consumed by curious individuals worldwide. Online communities exist where both skeptics and believers gather to share their own encounters with haunted dolls, adding to the ever-growing mythology and fascination surrounding these enigmatic objects.

The history of haunted dolls and their origins is a multifaceted and intriguing topic that combines history, folklore, and our innate human fascination with the supernatural. From ancient Egypt to the present day, haunted dolls have accompanied us through different cultures and time periods, leaving a lasting impression that challenges our understanding of the world. Whether one believes in the paranormal or views these stories as mere superstition, the allure of haunted dolls continues to captivate our imaginations, reminding us that even in the inanimate, there may be more than meets the eye.

Famous cases of haunted dolls throughout history

Throughout history, there have been intriguing accounts of haunted dolls that have captivated the human imagination. These dolls have evoked a range of emotions, from fear to fascination. Their alleged paranormal activities and the tales surrounding them have been documented in various sources. In this one, we will explore some of the famous cases of haunted dolls throughout history. By examining these compelling stories, we hope to unravel the mysteries surrounding these ethereal entities and gain a deeper understanding of the human fascination with the supernatural.

The Doll of Anne:

One of the most famous haunted dolls in history is the Doll of Anne, whose origins can be traced back to the 1800s. According to local legend, Anne was the cherished companion of a young girl named Emily. After Emily's untimely demise, the doll mysteriously disappeared. Years later, the doll reappeared in a small antique shop, catching the attention of a paranormal investigator. Upon acquiring the doll, the investigator reported experiencing strange phenomena such as unexplained movement and whispers. It seemed as though the spirit of Emily had attached itself to the Doll of Anne, seeking solace in its familiar presence. Many subsequent owners of the doll have reported eerie encounters, supporting the belief that the Doll of Anne is indeed haunted.

Robert the Doll:

Robert the Doll, another iconic haunted doll, has both fascinated and terrorized people for over a century. Originally owned by the Otto family, Robert was said to possess a malevolent spirit. Numerous reports describe how Robert would move on his own accord, change facial expressions, and emit eerie laughter. Witnesses claim that his eyes would follow them around the room and that his presence itself felt ominously unsettling. After his time with the Otto family, Robert the Doll was donated to a museum in Key West, where he still resides today. Visitors to the museum claim that if they take photographs or mock him, they experience a streak of bad luck or encounter other strange occurrences. Robert's unnerving presence continues to captivate the curiosity and fear of many who cross his path.

The Bride Doll:

The haunting tale of the Bride Doll is another captivating case that has endured through history. This doll, with its hauntingly beautiful features, was discovered in an abandoned wedding dress in a once-bustling New Orleans hotel. The origins of the doll remain shrouded in mystery, but rumors suggest that it was crafted in the image of a bride who met a tragic fate on her wedding day. The doll is said to exude an aura of sadness, often accompanied by disembodied cries and faint echoes of wedding hymns. Many visitors to the hotel claim that they have seen the doll move on its own and even witnessed her shedding tears. The Bride Doll serves as a chilling reminder of love lost and the lingering spirits of those who were denied their happily ever afters.

Okiku's Doll:

In Japan, the legend of Okiku's Doll has become an integral part of the country's cultural lore. This particular haunted doll is said to have been brought to the Mannenji temple in Hokkaido in the early 1900s. According to the story, a young girl named Okiku tragically passed away before her time. A doll was made in her likeness to comfort her grieving family. However, the spirit of Okiku seemingly infused itself within the doll, leading to inexplicable events. The doll's hair is said to grow on its own, and witnesses have reported hearing a child's laughter emanating from its tiny porcelain mouth. Today, Okiku's Doll is displayed in the temple, attracting visitors from around the world who come to witness its supernatural qualities firsthand.

HAUNTED DOLLS HAVE long captivated our imagination with their paranormal stories. These examples of the Doll of Anne, Robert the Doll, the Bride Doll, and Okiku's Doll are just a glimpse into the intriguing world of haunted dolls throughout history. While skeptics may dismiss these stories as mere fabrications or coincidences, it is undeniable that these accounts have left deep impressions on those who have encountered these dolls. Their tales continue to fascinate and inspire countless individuals to delve into the mysterious and unexplained. By exploring these cases, we gain a greater appreciation for the power of storytelling, the allure of the supernatural, and the enduring fascination with haunted dolls.

How the haunted doll curse has influenced horror culture

Among the myriad of terrifying themes in horror, the haunted doll curse, a concept deeply embedded in folklore, has emerged as a captivating and enduring fascination. In this exploration, we delve into the profound influence the haunted doll curse has exerted on horror culture, unraveling its origins, evolution, and impact on literature, movies, and popular folklore.

Origins of the Haunted Doll Curse:

The haunted doll curse traces its origins back to ancient times when people believed dolls possessed a spiritual essence. From ancient Egypt's magical figurines to European folklore's tales of cursed dolls, the concept of inanimate objects harboring malevolent spirits has thrived throughout history. However, widespread stories of dolls causing eerie happenings took root during the Victorian era, mainly due to the rise of spiritualism and the advent of the modern doll industry.

The Rise of the Haunted Doll Curse in Horror Literature:

It was the realm of literature where the haunted doll curse found a fertile ground to captivate readers. Dolls, intriguing objects that straddle the border between animate and inanimate, played a significant role in countless eerie narratives. Bram Stoker's "Dracula," for example, introduced the cryptic character of Vampira, a fanged, undead puppet, seducing readers with her unnerving presence.

However, it was with the publication of Robert Eugene Otto's memoir, "The Autobiography of Robert Eugene Otto and the Story of the Haunted Doll, 'Robert,'" that the haunted doll phenomenon truly captured the public's imagination. This memoir served as a catalyst, inspiring a myriad of chilling tales featuring enchanted or possessed dolls. Authors like R.L. Stine, Stephen King, and Ramsey Campbell seized upon this theme, weaving haunting tales that solidified the haunted doll curse's lasting prominence in horror literature.

Haunting the Silver Screen: Haunted Dolls in Cinema:

While literature set the foundation, cinema played a pivotal role in translating the eerie allure of haunted dolls into a visual medium. In 1963, "The Devil Doll" introduced audiences to the iconic voodoo doll trope, portraying its usage for revenge, bringing occultism into the limelight. Following this, horror classics like "Child's Play" (1988) and "Dolly Dearest" (1991) propelled the haunted doll curse into mainstream horror, fostering a significant evolution in the genre.

Moreover, the Japanese film "Ju-On: The Grudge" (2002) further expanded the haunted doll curse narrative, introducing the world to the infamous ghostly doll, Kayako, and her eerie shuffling movement. This film sparked a wave of Japanese and Korean horror movies featuring haunted dolls, imprinting this trope as a distinct hallmark of Asian horror cinema.

Consumer Culture and Haunted Doll Collecting:

Haunted dolls not only captivate audiences through media but also through the world of collectors. As the public fascination with the paranormal grew, so did an underground market for haunted dolls. Amateur paranormal enthusiasts and collectors began acquiring haunted dolls, hoping to experience the eerie and supernatural firsthand. This subculture, fed by online auction platforms and collector conventions, has not only bolstered the haunted doll curse's influence but also contributed significantly to its continued popularity.

Resilience in Popular Folklore:

The haunted doll curse has not only thrived within the realms of literature and film but also gained a permanent place in popular folklore. Numerous urban legends and eyewitness accounts of malevolent dolls circulating among communities have bolstered the belief in their menacing powers. Whether it be the infamous Annabelle doll or the stories of haunted dolls causing inexplicable phenomena, these tales circulate among friends, igniting fear and fascination.

THE HAUNTED DOLL CURSE has unquestionably left an indelible mark on horror culture, permeating literature, cinema, and popular folklore. Its origins intertwined with the annals of human history, this haunting trope taps into our fear of the unknown, the uncanny, and the supernatural. Evolving with the times, haunted dolls continue to captivate audiences and inspire storytellers, ensuring their enduring presence within the horror genre, where they will continue to haunt our nightmares for generations to come.

Chapter 16: The Phantom Hitchhiker Legend

THE DIFFERENT VARIATIONS of the Phantom Hitchhiker story

One of the most common variations of the Phantom Hitchhiker story revolves around a driver who picks up a hitchhiker on a dark and desolate road. The driver, unaware that the hitchhiker is a phantom, engages in a conversation with them, only to discover that the hitchhiker has disappeared from the car without a trace. The driver is left bewildered and terrified, unable to explain how the hitchhiker vanished. This variation often ends with the driver seeking out the location where they picked up the hitchhiker, only to find a grave or a memorial to someone who died at that spot years ago.

Another popular variation of the Phantom Hitchhiker story features a hitchhiker who is given a ride by a kind and benevolent driver. As they travel together, the hitchhiker shares a deeply personal and tragic story, recounting their untimely death and the reason why they continue to haunt the roads. In some versions, the driver offers to help the hitchhiker by fulfilling their last wish, whether it be delivering a message to a loved one or visiting a specific location. Once the driver fulfills the hitchhiker's request, they vanish, leaving behind a profound sense of closure and gratitude.

The Phantom Hitchhiker story also takes on different forms based on the cultural context in which it is retold. In some versions, the hitchhiker is a vengeful spirit seeking revenge for a past injustice. They target specific individuals who have wronged them or their loved ones, and the encounter with the hitchhiker serves as a warning or a punishment for their misdeeds.

This variation often incorporates elements of supernatural forces and the concept of karma, creating a chilling tale of justice and retribution.

Another cultural variation of the Phantom Hitchhiker story involves the hitchhiker being a harbinger of death or disaster. They appear to unsuspecting drivers, foretelling an imminent tragedy that will befall them or their loved ones. This variation often instills a sense of urgency and fear in the listener, as they grapple with the knowledge that the hitchhiker's appearance signifies an impending catastrophe that cannot be avoided.

It is worth noting that the Phantom Hitchhiker story has been adapted and modernized with the evolution of technology. In recent years, there have been variations that involve ghostly hitchhikers appearing in rideshare vehicles or haunted GPS navigation systems. These contemporary adaptations tap into the fears and anxieties associated with the reliance on technology and the unknown dangers it can bring.

Despite the variations and cultural nuances, one common theme that permeates all versions of the Phantom Hitchhiker story is the element of the supernatural. Whether the hitchhiker is a benevolent spirit seeking closure or a malevolent entity wreaking havoc, their presence and subsequent disappearance defy rational explanation. This supernatural element adds a layer of mystery and intrigue to the story, captivating the audience and leaving them with a sense of wonder and unease. From vengeful spirits seeking justice to benevolent ghosts in need of closure, this urban legend continues to captivate the imaginations of those who hear it. Each variation offers a unique twist on the theme of a vanishing hitchhiker, adding to the overall mystique and allure of the story. Whether you believe in the supernatural or not, the Phantom Hitchhiker story serves as a reminder of the enduring power of folklore and the human fascination with the unknown.

The psychological reasons behind the Phantom Hitchhiker phenomenon

One key psychological concept that sheds light on the Phantom Hitchhiker phenomenon is that of expectation and selective attention. As human beings, we are prone to interpretation biases, meaning that we often perceive and remember events in a way that aligns with our pre-existing beliefs and expectations. In the case of encountering a ghostly figure on the roadside, our brains may actively seek out and amplify any signs or clues that affirm our belief in the supernatural. This can lead to the creation of vivid and detailed recollections, particularly when combined with the power of suggestibility and shared social narratives.

Another influential psychological factor in understanding the Phantom Hitchhiker phenomenon is the human desire for a sense of mystery and transcendence. We are naturally drawn to experiences that challenge our everyday perceptions and offer a glimpse into a world beyond our own. The Phantom Hitchhiker narrative taps into this longing, providing individuals with a thrilling and extraordinary encounter that defies rational explanation. By embracing the story of the supernatural hitchhiker, individuals can momentarily escape the mundane and open themselves up to the possibility of a hidden, enchanting realm.

Furthermore, the Phantom Hitchhiker legend serves as a means for individuals to explore and express their own fears and anxieties. Picking up a hitchhiker, a stranger in need, is an act of trust and vulnerability. The spectral nature of the phantom hitchhiker amplifies these feelings, transforming the encounter into a potent symbol of our deepest fears – the unknown, the transient nature of life, and the uncertainty of what lies ahead. By engaging with this legend, individuals can confront and navigate these emotions within the safe confines of a supernatural tale.

The psychological reasons behind the popularity and longevity of the Phantom Hitchhiker phenomenon can also be linked to the power of storytelling and collective belief systems. Throughout history, stories have played a fundamental role in shaping cultures and societies, conveying shared values, and imparting wisdom. Legends, myths, and supernatural tales have the ability to bind communities together, fostering a shared history and a collective identity. The Phantom Hitchhiker narrative serves as a cultural touchstone, connecting individuals across generations and geographical boundaries. By passing down and retelling the story, we establish a sense of continuity and preserve the intangible essence of our cultural heritage.

While the psychological explanations for the Phantom Hitchhiker phenomenon provide valuable insights into the narrative's endurance and popularity, it is important to recognize that they do not negate the possibility of genuine extraordinary experiences. While many encounters may indeed be based on misperception, expectation biases, and the power of storytelling, it would be remiss to discount the potential existence of genuine paranormal encounters altogether. The complexity of the human experience, the limitations of our understanding, and the vastness of the universe offer fertile ground for unexplained phenomena. From our inherent biases and expectations to the allure of mystery and the exploration of our fears and anxieties, the phenomenon provides an intriguing context for understanding the complex workings of the human mind. By delving into the psychological underpinnings of this supernatural legend, we gain a greater appreciation for the power of storytelling, the significance of collective beliefs, and the enduring intrigue of the unknown. Whether fueled by psychology or genuine paranormal experiences, the Phantom Hitchhiker phenomenon continues to captivate and enchant us, offering a window into the profound depths of the human psyche.

Real-life encounters with the Phantom Hitchhiker

In this exploration, we delve into real-life anecdotes of those brave souls who have experienced these ethereal beings firsthand. Drawing from extensive research and eyewitness accounts, we aim to shed light on this captivating phenomenon that has captivated generations. Join us on this quest to unravel the secrets behind the enigmatic Phantom Hitchhiker.

Legends and Lore of the Phantom Hitchhiker

The phenomenon of the Phantom Hitchhiker has permeated human folklore for centuries. Ancient tales from diverse cultures resonate with similar themes — hitchhikers appearing on deserted roads, pleading for a lift, but vanishing mysteriously during the journey. These tales offer profound connections to our collective psyche and tap into our fascination with the unknown. We explore the roots of this phenomenon, tracing its origin to mythologies, folktales, and supernatural beliefs across different cultures and time periods.

Analyzing the Psychological Aspects

Embarking on a psychological exploration, we delve into the minds of those who claim to have encountered the Phantom Hitchhiker. By examining various theories, such as the power of suggestion, sleep paralysis, and the uncanny valley, we aim to understand the human psyche's susceptibility to such apparitions. Our analysis will help uncover the psychological and emotional factors that contribute to the perceived experiences and the lasting impact they may have on individuals.

The Intersection of Science and the Paranormal

Moving beyond folklore and psychology, we venture into the realm of science to examine the plausibility of the Phantom Hitchhiker phenomenon. Can it be explained by physical and natural laws known to us. By drawing upon quantum physics, neuroscience, and the extensive field of paranormal studies, we strive to offer scientific insights that may shed light on the nature of these spectral encounters. We aim to bridge the gap between the measurable world and the metaphysical, opening doors for a greater understanding of the unexplained.

Resonating Experiences: Shared Encounters

Within this one, we present a collection of firsthand accounts from those who have encountered the Phantom Hitchhiker. These authentic and remarkable stories provide glimpses into the diversity of experiences and the profound impact they have had on individuals. Through the lenses of these encounters, we uncover common threads, symbolic elements, and the significance of the Phantom Hitchhiker's presence in our lives. These personal narratives serve as a compelling testament to the enduring power of these encounters.

Cultural and Historical Significance

The Phantom Hitchhiker is not merely a supernatural phenomenon; it also acts as a mirror reflecting the societies in which these tales emerge. From ancient folklore to contemporary urban legends, we analyze how the cultural, historical, and societal contexts shape the perception and interpretation of these apparitions. By examining regional variations, cultural rituals, and historical events, we gain a nuanced appreciation for the Phantom Hitchhiker's resonance across different time periods and cultures.

AS WE CONCLUDE OUR exploration into the world of the Phantom Hitchhiker, we remain awestruck by the profound impact these encounters have on both individuals and society as a whole. By examining their origins, psychological implications, scientific plausibility, personal narratives, and cultural significances, we have unraveled some of the veiled mysteries shrouded by this ethereal phenomenon. Whether a believer or skeptic, there is no denying the enigmatic allure of the Phantom Hitchhiker and its enduring presence in our collective imagination.

Chapter 17: The Poltergeist Phenomenon

THE HISTORY OF POLTERGEIST activity and research

To fully appreciate the history of poltergeist activity, we must trace its roots back to ancient times, where mention of paranormal phenomena can be found in numerous cultures. The term "poltergeist" itself is derived from the German words "poltern," meaning to make noise or racket, and "geist," translating to ghost or spirit. Such disturbances were often attributed to mischievous or vengeful spirits, believed to be the souls of deceased individuals seeking revenge or attention. These beliefs were prevalent in cultures from ancient Greece and Rome to medieval Europe.

In the 19th century, the study of poltergeist phenomena took on a more scientific approach. Researchers began documenting cases of inexplicable disturbances, focusing on the reported physical and auditory manifestations associated with these events. The investigations aimed to separate fact from fiction and gain a deeper understanding of this perplexing phenomenon. During this time, notable cases such as the "Bell Witch" in Tennessee and the "Great Amherst Mystery" in Canada garnered considerable attention, propelling the study of poltergeists into the mainstream consciousness.

In the early 20th century, pioneers in psychical research, such as the Society for Psychical Research (SPR), rigorously investigated poltergeist activity. These researchers employed scientific methods, including surveying witnesses, conducting interviews, and collecting physical evidence to shed light on these seemingly inexplicable occurrences. Their work laid the foundation for a more systematic and evidence-based approach to studying poltergeists, breaking away from the superstitious beliefs of earlier times. Despite their efforts, however, definitive explanations for poltergeist phenomena remained elusive.

More recent advances in technology have allowed researchers to explore poltergeist activity with a greater level of precision and objectivity. The advent of modern recording devices, such as cameras and audio recorders, has enabled investigators to capture and document purported poltergeist manifestations. These technological tools, combined with sophisticated data analysis techniques, have allowed for a more comprehensive examination of this perplexing phenomenon. However, the interpretation of these collected data remains subjective, and skepticism continues to challenge the validity of poltergeist claims.

One potential explanation for poltergeist activity lies in the field of parapsychology, which investigates the paranormal and psychic phenomena. Parapsychologists propose that some cases of poltergeists could be attributed to psychokinetic abilities, where an individual unconsciously channels their emotional energy, resulting in the observed disturbances. This theory suggests that individuals experiencing high levels of emotional stress or trauma may inadvertently manifest poltergeist-like phenomena without conscious intention. While intriguing, the psychokinetic hypothesis remains controversial and lacks conclusive empirical evidence.

Another avenue of research focuses on the psychological and environmental factors that may contribute to poltergeist activity. Some experts suggest that cases of purported poltergeists could be manifestations of repressed or unconscious psychodynamic processes. In this view, individuals experiencing unresolved psychological conflicts may unconsciously project their inner turmoil into the physical world, giving rise to the perceptible disturbances commonly associated with poltergeist activity. Environmental factors, such as geomagnetic anomalies or infrasound, have also been proposed as potential triggers for these phenomena. However, further research is needed to validate or discredit these theories definitively.

The history of poltergeist activity and research is a rich tapestry interwoven with folklore, scientific inquiry, and unexplained phenomena. From ancient legends to cutting-edge scientific investigations, our quest to understand poltergeists continues to captivate and challenge our perceptions of reality. As we strive to unlock the secrets of these elusive entities, we must approach the subject with an open mind, rigorous scientific methodology, and an appreciation for the deep cultural and historical roots that have shaped our understanding of this enigmatic phenomenon.

Theories about the nature of poltergeists

One prevalent theory suggests that poltergeists are not external entities or spirits, but rather manifestations of the unconscious mind. This theory draws inspiration from the field of psychology and psychoanalysis. According to this perspective, individuals experiencing poltergeist activity may be harboring deep-seated emotional turmoil or unresolved psychological conflicts. These repressed emotions and conflicts then find an outlet through the physical disturbances that are commonly associated with poltergeist phenomena.

Supporters of the psychological theory argue that the individuals experiencing poltergeist activity are often teenagers going through puberty or individuals in stressful life situations. They hypothesize that the heightened emotional state during these periods of life can trigger the release of unconscious energy, leading to the unexplained movements of objects. Additionally, proponents of this theory often point to the fact that poltergeist activity tends to center around a particular person, rather than a specific location, further suggesting a psychological cause.

Another theory about the nature of poltergeists revolves around the concept of residual energy or psychic imprinting. This theory posits that certain locations or objects can absorb and retain energy from past events, creating a sort of playback or reenactment of these events at a later time. In the case of poltergeist activity, this residual energy is said to be released, resulting in the movement or displacement of objects.

Advocates of this theory argue that poltergeist phenomena often occur in places with a history of traumatic events or emotional intensity, such as old houses or battlefields. They believe that the emotional energy associated with these events becomes imprinted on the environment and can be triggered or released under certain conditions. This theory offers an intriguing explanation for poltergeist activity, as it suggests that the phenomena may be less about external entities and more about the residual energy left behind by previous events.

A third theory posits that poltergeist activity is the result of external entities or spirits. This theory is rooted in traditional beliefs and folklore, which have long associated poltergeists with malevolent or mischievous spirits. According to this perspective, poltergeist phenomena are caused by the influence of spirits or entities that have somehow made a connection to the physical world.

Supporters of the spiritual theory argue that the unexplained movements of objects and phenomena associated with poltergeists cannot be solely attributed to internal psychological factors or residual energy. They believe that the external influence of spirits or entities is necessary to explain the nature and characteristics of poltergeist activity. This theory draws connections to paranormal investigations and the belief in supernatural entities.

It is important to note that none of these theories have been definitively proven or universally accepted by the scientific community. The nature of poltergeists remains a subject of ongoing research and speculation. However, the study of poltergeist phenomena provides a valuable window into the intersection of psychology, spirituality, and the unexplained. By considering these various theories, we can continue to enhance our understanding of these mysterious occurrences and their potential implications for our understanding of the world. Whether rooted in the depths of the human mind, residual energy from past events, or the influence of external spirits, the study of poltergeists is a testament to the enduring mystery and fascination that surrounds the supernatural realm.

Chapter 18: The Moaning Myrtle Legend

THE ORIGINS OF THE Moaning Myrtle ghost story

Moaning Myrtle, whose real name is Myrtle Elizabeth Warren, is introduced to readers in the second book of the Harry Potter series, "Harry Potter and the Chamber of Secrets." She is known for her incessant moaning and her tendency to haunt a particular bathroom in Hogwarts, which becomes a central location in the story. Although Myrtle's backstory is not fully explored in the books, Rowling drops hints that allow us to piece together her origins.

According to the books, Myrtle was a student at Hogwarts during the 1940s. As we dig deeper into her story, we discover that her death has a direct connection to the Chamber of Secrets, the hidden underground chamber at Hogwarts that becomes a focal point of the second book. As Hermione Granger's research reveals, Myrtle died after encountering Tom Riddle's basilisk, a giant snake. The basilisk, controlled by Tom Riddle (later known as Lord Voldemort), petrified Myrtle with its gaze, leading to her untimely demise.

Myrtle's tragic death becomes the catalyst for her transformation into a ghost. Her debut appearance in the bathroom scene, where Harry Potter first encounters her, reinforces the notion that she is tied to that specific location. It is believed that Myrtle chose to haunt that bathroom because it was the place of her death, allowing her to remain connected to the living world and, in some way, seek vengeance for her unfortunate demise.

Despite her grumpy and mischievous nature, Myrtle's personality gives us insights into her character. She is portrayed as someone who constantly seeks attention and craves empathy. Myrtle's incessant sobbing and moaning can be seen as a cry for help or a plea for recognition, as she feels ignored by her peers due to her nerdy and meek persona during her lifetime. This yearning for companionship manifests when she latches onto Harry and his friends, following them around and even revealing secrets to them.

Adding more layers to the story, the origins of the ghost's name are worth exploring. In an interview, J.K. Rowling mentioned that she named Moaning Myrtle after one of her childhood classmates. This playful nod by Rowling demonstrates how she draws inspiration from real-life experiences to craft her fictional universe. Furthermore, the alliteration in Myrtle's name adds to its memorable quality, making her character stand out in the minds of readers.

In the broader context of Hogwarts' history, Moaning Myrtle's presence adds depth to the school's lore. Hogwarts, despite its enchanting facade, has witnessed its fair share of tragedy and dark secrets throughout the centuries. Myrtle's untimely death is just one of the many unfortunate events that have occurred within its hallowed halls. This serves as a reminder that even in a world of magic and wonder, darkness and sorrow can still find their way in.

As readers delve into the origins of the Moaning Myrtle ghost story, they are left with a sense of empathy for the character. Myrtle's tragic death and her subsequent haunting of Hogwarts' bathrooms reveal the depths of human emotion and the longing for recognition, even in the afterlife. Rowling's masterful storytelling allows us to understand Myrtle's motivations and creates a nuanced and relatable ghost character that adds richness and complexity to the world of Harry Potter. Though her origin story is not fully fleshed out, the clues and hints dropped throughout the series provide enough material for readers to form their own understanding of Moaning Myrtle and her haunting presence in the Harry Potter universe.

A comparison between Moaning Myrtle and other famous ghost tales

Moaning Myrtle, a ghost haunting the second-floor girls' lavatory at Hogwarts School of Witchcraft and Wizardry, is a memorable character in the Harry Potter series. Rowling's creation manages to blend a touch of tragedy with a hint of humor, making her both relatable and endearing to readers. Myrtle's backstory, involving her untimely death in the very bathroom she now haunts, adds a layer of sympathy to her character. Her moaning and wailing, amplified by the echo of the lavatory, make her a distinctive figure in the Hogwarts grounds. This unique characterization sets her apart from other famous ghosts, whose stories may not carry the same touching blend of tragedy and humor.

One compelling aspect of comparing Moaning Myrtle to other famous ghost tales lies in the diverse cultural representation of these ethereal spirits. From classic literature to folklore and mythology, ghost stories have been told across centuries and across the globe. A familiar figure in English literature is the ghost of Hamlet's father, haunting the castle of Elsinore. This ghostly apparition, seeking vengeance for his unjust death, shares a common motive with Moaning Myrtle. Both ghosts have unfinished business that keeps them tethered to the world of the living, roaming the spaces that were once familiar to them. While notable differences exist, such as the circumstances of their deaths and their roles in the respective stories, examining these distinct ghosts highlights the broader themes and archetypes that permeate ghost tales worldwide.

Another potent avenue for comparison lies in the impact that these ghost stories have on their respective narratives. In many tales, ghosts serve as catalysts for character development and plot advancement. Moaning Myrtle, for instance, plays a crucial role in the Harry Potter series, acting as an informant to the young wizard trio when they need information about the Chamber of Secrets. Her interactions with the main characters provide critical clues that guide them in their endeavors. Similarly, in Charles Dickens's "A Christmas Carol," the iconic ghost of Ebenezer Scrooge's former business partner, Jacob Marley, sets the stage for the protagonist's transformation. Marley's haunting visitations provoke self-reflection and guide Scrooge's journey towards redemption. By examining the roles ghosts play in these stories, we gain valuable insights into how these ethereal beings function as storytellers' tools to advance narratives and deepen character development.

Beyond her literary impact, Moaning Myrtle's character offers a unique perspective on the theme of death and its connection to the living. Her presence reflects the ongoing influence that departed souls can have on the world of the living. Myrtle's loneliness and yearning for human companionship, despite being dead, emphasizes the enduring impact of her death, both emotionally and spiritually. This portrayal presents an opportunity to delve into the cultural and philosophical aspects of ghost stories. Across different tales and traditions, the portrayal of ghostly apparitions often reflects societies' beliefs and attitudes towards death and the afterlife. By exploring Moaning Myrtle's story alongside other ghost tales, we can analyze the interplay between cultural beliefs, narrative purposes, and the broader themes of mortality and the human condition. Moaning Myrtle, with her tragic yet relatable backstory and her blend of humor and melancholy, stands out as a memorable ghost in the Harry Potter series. By placing her story in conversation with other renowned ghost stories, we gain insights into the diverse cultural representations of apparitions, the narrative impact of such characters, and the exploration of death and the human condition. Through this analysis, we navigate the mystical realm of ghost tales while deepening our appreciation for the captivating and timeless nature of these ethereal beings.

The impact of Moaning Myrtle on the Harry Potter series

Moaning Myrtle, first introduced in "Harry Potter and the Chamber of Secrets," is a ghost haunting the second-floor girls' bathroom at Hogwarts School of Witchcraft and Wizardry. Her melancholic nature and constant lamentations make her a rather peculiar and intriguing character. Rowling expertly utilizes her presence to enhance the overall atmosphere of the series, provoking both sympathy and curiosity from readers. Myrtle's presence in the haunted bathroom adds an element of mystery and foreboding to the school, keeping readers on edge throughout the story.

One of the crucial impacts of Moaning Myrtle is her role in unlocking the secret of the Chamber of Secrets, a crucial plot point in the second book. When Harry Potter and his friends discover Myrtle's demise was a result of the opening of the Chamber of Secrets fifty years prior, they embark on a quest to solve the mystery. Myrtle becomes an essential guide, providing crucial clues and insights to assist our heroes in their exploration. Her connection to the events of the past and her willingness to help adds depth to the plot, engaging readers with a sense of urgency, the desire to uncover the truth, and the impending danger that lurks within the school's walls.

Additionally, Moaning Myrtle's impact extends beyond her role in unraveling mysteries. She also serves as a source of comfort and understanding for characters burdened by loneliness and isolation. Throughout the series,

Myrtle offers solace to Harry and others who seek her company. Harry, who experiences numerous tribulations, finds solace in conversing with Myrtle, as she's a constant presence with whom he can confide his worries and fears. Despite her occasional irritability, Myrtle's compassionate nature is infectious, making her an unexpected ally during times of hardship.

Furthermore, Moaning Myrtle's character provides a deeper exploration of the theme of mortality present in the Harry Potter series. As a ghost, she is caught between the realms of the living and the dead, forever trapped in a state of limbo. This existential crisis that follows Myrtle adds a layer of complexity to the story, allowing readers to ponder on the consequences of actions and their impact on individuals long after they are gone. Myrtle serves as a reminder that life is fleeting and choices have lasting consequences. Her character raises thought-provoking questions about the nature of existence, leaving readers with profound takeaways amidst the fantastical world of witches and wizards. J.K. Rowling skillfully crafts a character whose presence resonates throughout the pages of the books. Moaning Myrtle adds an air of mystery and foreboding to the narrative, unlocking secrets crucial to the plot's development. However, it is her role in providing solace, exploring themes of mortality, and adding depth to the story that truly solidifies her importance. With her unique qualities and undeniable charm, Moaning Myrtle leaves an emotional and intellectual impact on readers, elevating the overall narrative of the Harry Potter series to new heights.

Chapter 19: The Black Volga Myth

THE URBAN LEGEND OF the Black Volga car

To truly understand the allure of the Black Volga legend, we must first examine its origins. While the specific details may vary from one telling to another, the story often begins in Eastern Europe during the mid-twentieth century. It is said that a black luxury car, usually identified as a Volga, would cruise the streets, driven by a mysterious and malevolent figure. The car's purpose was to abduct unsuspecting individuals, who would then vanish without a trace. This legend began circulating during a time of political unrest and social unease, which undoubtedly contributed to its widespread popularity. The fear of the unknown and the fascination with the unexplained drew people in, making the Black Volga a subject of both fascination and dread.

As with many urban legends, the specifics of the Black Volga story differ depending on the cultural context in which it is told. In some versions, the car is linked to an organized criminal group or a secret government agency, suggesting a more sinister purpose behind the abductions. Other tellings focus on the supernatural, proposing that the driver of the Black Volga is a demonic figure or even the personification of Death itself. These variations illustrate how urban legends adapt and evolve to suit the fears and beliefs of different communities. The Black Volga becomes a vessel for collective anxieties, serving as a cautionary tale and a reflection of deep-seated societal fears.

What is particularly fascinating about the Black Volga legend is its longevity and its international reach. Similar tales of sinister vehicles have been reported in various countries, from Russia to Hungary, from Mexico to the United States. The details may differ, but the underlying themes remain consistent: a dark vehicle, a driver with nefarious intent, and a sense of foreboding. This global spread speaks to the universal nature of human fears and the power of storytelling to transcend cultural boundaries. The legend of the Black Volga taps into our primordial apprehensions, instinctively resonating with audiences around the world.

But why do urban legends like the Black Volga continue to captivate us. Why do we eagerly pass these stories on, even when we know they are likely nothing more than fanciful tales. The answer lies in the psychological appeal of these narratives. Urban legends provide a way to explore our fears in a controlled environment, allowing us to experience a thrill without real danger. They offer an escape from the monotony of everyday life, a chance to engage with something extraordinary and uncanny. By sharing these stories with others, we form connections and create a sense of community. The Black Volga legend becomes a shared experience, a common thread that binds people together and reinforces our shared humanity.

Moreover, the urban legend of the Black Volga serves a cultural function. It reflects the anxieties and concerns of the societies in which it thrives. During times of political upheaval, economic uncertainty, or social unrest, legends like this emerge as a way to process and express our collective fears. By externalizing our worries onto a malevolent car or a phantom figure, we gain a sense of control over our fears. We personify the unknown, creating a tangible enemy that we can face, even if only in our imaginations. The Black Volga becomes a symbol of the dangers lurking in our modern world, a cautionary reminder of the ever-present perils that we must remain vigilant against. Through examining its origins, variations, and psychological appeal, we can gain a deeper understanding of the cultural and psychological significance of urban legends as a whole. While the truth behind the Black Volga remains elusive, the power of the legend persists. It reveals the enduring allure of the unknown, the enduring power of storytelling, and the eternal desire to explore the realms of the extraordinary. In unraveling this dark and mysterious tale, we embark on a journey into the collective imagination, discovering the depths of human fears and aspirations.

Historical context and background of the Black Volga myth

To fully grasp the historical context of the Black Volga myth, one must first delve into the tumultuous era in which it emerged. The myth gained prominence during the early Soviet Union, when the country was undergoing significant societal changes. Rapid industrialization, urbanization, and the consequences of the Bolshevik Revolution were reshaping everyday life. This period was marked by widespread poverty, power struggles, and a pervasive sense of uncertainty. As a result, people sought explanations for the challenges that plagued their communities, and folklore and urban legends filled this void.

The Black Volga myth, said to be a manifestation of the negative aspects of the Soviet regime, reflects the anxieties and fears of the time. The notorious black car was commonly associated with secret police or government officials preying on innocent citizens. It symbolized the oppressive nature of the Soviet regime, instilling a sense of terror and paranoia among the population. The myth also tapped into the very real issue of child abductions, which were on the rise during this period due to social unrest and a lack of effective law enforcement.

Furthermore, the Black Volga myth can be seen as a reflection of pre-existing cultural beliefs and superstitions. In Russian folklore, the color black often represents death, darkness, and evil forces. By attaching these attributes to the mythological car, storytellers were able to tap into deep-rooted cultural fears, making the story more plausible and terrifying. Additionally, the concept of a malevolent entity luring and abducting children has been a recurring theme in numerous folklores around the world, serving as a cautionary tale to both children and adults.

The Black Volga myth grew in prominence thanks to its dissemination through oral tradition and the media. With Russia's vast and diverse geography, each region developed its own variation of the story, adapting it to fit local circumstances. Some versions included specific details about the appearance of the car or the methods used by its occupants, further contributing to the urban legend's mystique. In an era without widespread access to information, people relied heavily on rumors and hearsay, making it easier for the myth to take root and spread.

Like many urban legends, the Black Volga myth also served as a cautionary tale, reinforcing societal norms and values. Parents warned their children about the dangers of talking to strangers or wandering alone at night, painting the black car as a metaphorical embodiment of these risks. This moralistic aspect of the myth provided a framework for education and socialization, while simultaneously perpetuating a collective apprehension surrounding the unknown.

As time went on, the Black Volga myth evolved and adapted to changing times. With the fall of the Soviet Union and the subsequent transition to a market economy, the myth lost some of its power as societal fears shifted. However, its legacy has endured, as it continues to be referenced in popular culture, urban explorations, and discussions about folklore and urban legends. The myth tapped into the fears and anxieties of a society in flux, symbolizing the oppressive nature of the Soviet regime and reflecting pre-existing cultural beliefs. Through oral tradition and media dissemination, the myth took on distinct regional variations, growing in prominence and serving as a cautionary tale. While its influence has waned in recent years, the Black Volga myth remains an intriguing example of how folklore and urban legends can capture the imagination and reflect societal concerns.

Possible explanations for the origins of the tale

The origins of a tale are often shrouded in mystery, leaving us intrigued and curious about their beginnings. Throughout history, countless stories have captivated audiences, passed down through generations, and become a cornerstone of various cultures. While pinning down the exact origins of a tale can be challenging, scholars and researchers have proposed several possible explanations that shed light on their creation and evolution. In this exploration, we will delve into ancient folklore, cultural influences, and the universal human experience to gain a better understanding of the possible origins of these captivating tales.

One possible explanation for the origins of a tale lies in ancient folklore and mythology. Folklore has been an integral part of human culture since time immemorial, holding a mirror to the values, beliefs, and fears of our ancestors. Tales often draw inspiration from mythological creatures, gods, and legendary figures, intertwining human experiences with fantastical elements. For instance, the tale of King Arthur and the Knights of the Round Table, which has enchanted audiences for centuries, is believed to have roots in Celtic mythology and the Arthurian legends. By exploring ancient folklore, we can uncover the contextual influences that shaped these tales and connect them to their distant origins.

Cultural influences have also played a significant role in shaping the origins of a tale. Stories often reflect the values, customs, and ideals unique to a specific culture or community. Folktales from the East, such as the Arabian Nights, offer a glimpse into the rich and diverse tapestry of Middle Eastern cultures. These tales, with their magical landscapes and colorful characters, carry the imprint of the cultures they emerged from. The origins of such tales may lie in oral storytelling traditions, where they were passed down through generations, adding nuances and adaptations as they traveled across regions and time. By analyzing the cultural influences on a tale, we can discern the societal aspirations, moral lessons, and historical events that contributed to its creation.

Another explanation for the origins of a tale lies in the universal human experience. Tales often explore fundamental aspects of the human condition, serving as a form of collective catharsis or guidance. Stories like Hansel and Gretel or Little Red Riding Hood touch upon primal fears, cautionary tales, and the human instinct for survival. They tap into universal themes such as the struggle against evil, personal growth, and the triumph of good over bad. The origins of these tales may stem from shared experiences, fears, and triumphs that are inherently human. By examining the universal aspects of a tale, we can uncover the common threads that bind us together and offer insight into the essence of storytelling itself.

Furthermore, the origins of a tale can often be attributed to the creative ingenuity of individuals. Many famous tales have been attributed to specific authors or storytellers who crafted them based on their imagination, experiences, or personal beliefs. Take the beloved tales of the Brothers Grimm, who took inspiration from German folklore and composed their own versions of popular stories such as Cinderella or Snow White. Similarly, Hans Christian Andersen wrote countless enchanting fairy tales that continue to enchant readers worldwide. These authors drew upon their surroundings, observations, and cultural context, establishing their tales as enduring classics. Exploring the individuals behind a tale can shed light on the personal motivations, literary influences, and creativity that brought these stories to life. By examining these various factors, we can piece together the puzzle of how these captivating stories came into existence. Whether rooted in ancient mythology, shaped by cultural context, or grounded in universal themes, tales continue to hold the power to captivate, entertain, and teach. Unraveling their origins allows us to appreciate the artistry, legacy, and timeless appeal of these cherished narratives.

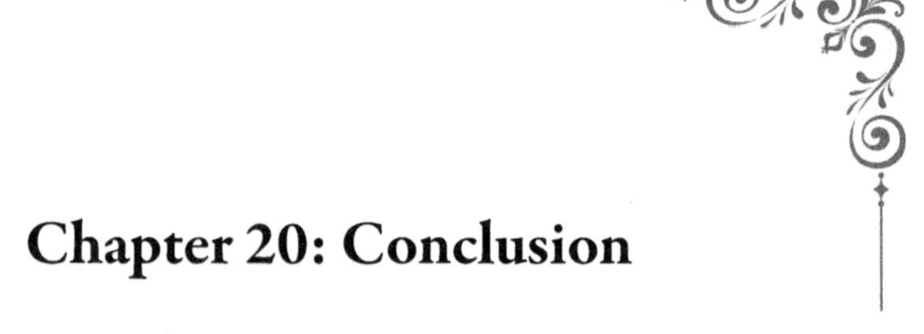

Chapter 20: Conclusion

THE ENDURING APPEAL of urban legends

One key factor that contributes to the enduring appeal of urban legends is their ability to tap into our deep-rooted fears and anxieties. These stories often touch upon common human worries such as the fear of the unknown, death, supernatural forces, or simply the unexpected. By addressing these fears, urban legends provide a platform for people to connect and share their own experiences, helping them make sense of the world around them. Urban legends can function as a form of catharsis, allowing individuals to confront their fears in a safe, controlled manner. This psychological aspect of urban legends creates a common ground for people to come together, forming a sense of community and shared experiences.

Furthermore, urban legends often contain elements of mystery and intrigue, which is another aspect contributing to their lasting appeal. Humans have an inherent curiosity for the unknown, and urban legends feed into this curiosity by presenting stories that challenge our understanding of the world. These tales often involve unsolved mysteries, unexplained events, or bizarre occurrences that pique our interest and leave us wanting to know more. The ambiguity surrounding these legends adds an element of suspense, drawing in the listener or reader with each twist and turn. This sense of anticipation and fascination keeps urban legends alive as they continue to circulate and be retold across different generations.

In addition to the psychological and mysterious aspects, urban legends also tap into our social nature. Humans are social creatures who thrive on connection and communication, and urban legends provide an excellent opportunity for storytelling and shared experiences. These stories are often passed on through informal channels, such as gatherings, family reunions, or online forums, where individuals come together to exchange narratives. This oral tradition allows urban legends to take on a life of their own as they are customized and adapted by each teller. The act of retelling these stories not only strengthens the bond between individuals but also solidifies the legend's place in the collective memory of a community.

Moreover, the cultural context within which urban legends arise contributes to their enduring appeal. These stories often reflect the anxieties, aspirations, and values of a particular society. Urban legends can illuminate deeper societal fears, such as the fear of technology, corruption, or societal breakdown. They can also reflect societal changes, adapting to advancements in technology and the changing landscape of modern life. By examining the themes and motifs within urban legends, researchers gain insights into the cultural and societal zeitgeist of a specific time and place. This cultural relevance helps urban legends maintain their appeal as they become artifacts of collective memory that encapsulate unique moments in history.

It is worth noting that advancements in technology, with the rise of the internet and social media, have amplified the reach and impact of urban legends. Previously confined to local communities or specific regions, urban legends can now spread rapidly on a global scale. The digital age has facilitated the easy dissemination of these stories, allowing them to reach a much broader audience and evolve more rapidly through online platforms. Additionally, the interactive nature of social media encourages the sharing and discussion of urban legends, keeping them relevant and engaging. This interconnectedness has further contributed to the enduring appeal and longevity of urban legends. These stories captivate us by providing a means to confront our fears, satisfy our curiosity for the unknown, and engage in shared experiences. Urban legends allow us to explore the boundaries of our understanding and connect with others, forming a lasting bond. As technology advances and society evolves, urban legends continue to adapt and thrive, captivating new generations and reminding us of the enduring power of storytelling in our lives.

Lessons learned from exploring famous urban myths

One prevalent urban myth that has captured the fascination of people for centuries is the tale of the Loch Ness Monster. Deep within the vast, mysterious waters of Scotland's Loch Ness, the myth tells of a large aquatic creature, described as a plesiosaur-like beast, lurking beneath the surface. While countless individuals have claimed to witness the creature, its existence continues to remain a subject of debate among scientists and skeptics. However, the enduring popularity of the Loch Ness Monster myth provides us with a vital lesson on the power of imagination and the allure of the unknown. The idea of a hidden creature in the depths of a lake taps into our primal curiosity, reminding us of the mysteries that still exist in the world and inviting us to embrace the wonders that lie beyond our comprehension.

Another urban myth that has gained widespread attention is the story of the Slender Man. Born on internet forums and portrayed as a tall, faceless figure clad in a black suit, the Slender Man myth transcended its digital origins. It insidiously infiltrated popular culture and triggered a series of alarming events, including a violent attack, demonstrating the potential dangers that can arise from blurring the boundaries between fiction and reality. However, the Slender Man phenomenon imparts upon us the importance of critical thinking and media literacy in the digital age. By engaging with this myth, we are reminded of the responsibility we have to question and evaluate the sources of information we encounter, ensuring we approach them with a discerning eye and a healthy dose of skepticism.

Moving to the realm of haunted folklore, the legend of the Amityville Horror holds a prominent place. It originated from the infamous events that allegedly occurred in a house in Amityville, New York, where a family was said to have been terrorized by supernatural forces. This urban myth, which spawned numerous books and films, serves as a powerful reminder of the sway that storytelling can have on our perception of reality. Despite the questionable veracity of the events, the Amityville Horror myth carries with it the lesson of how narratives can shape our collective consciousness. It teaches us to examine the influence of stories on our beliefs, highlighting the importance of critical analysis and independent thinking to avoid falling prey to sensationalism and unsubstantiated claims.

Additionally, the urban legend surrounding the lost city of Atlantis has captured our collective imagination for centuries. Often depicted as a utopian civilization that vanished beneath the sea, Atlantis serves as both a cautionary tale and a source of inspiration. The myth reminds us of the fragility of even the greatest civilizations, urging us to reflect upon the importance of environmental stewardship and the potential consequences of our actions. Furthermore, the allure of Atlantis encourages us to embrace the potentials of exploration and discovery, pushing the boundaries of human knowledge and pursuing dreams that may seem unattainable.

As we delve into the lessons learned from exploring famous urban myths, it becomes evident that these narratives hold a wealth of insights that extend beyond mere entertainment. From the exploration of the Loch Ness Monster myth, we learn to embrace the unknown and nurture our curiosity. The tale of the Slender Man reminds us of the necessity of critical thinking and media literacy in navigating the digital landscape. The Amityville Horror myth serves as a cautionary tale about the power of storytelling and our susceptibility to its influence. To draw to a close, the legend of Atlantis prompts us to reflect on the fragility of civilizations and the importance of exploration and preservation. These myths, spanning from the Loch Ness Monster to Slender Man, from Amityville Horror to Atlantis, teach us to embrace the wonders of the unknown while approaching information with skepticism and critical thinking. They urge us to consider the impact of storytelling on our beliefs and encourage us to reflect upon the consequences of our actions. So, let us embark on this venture to uncover the hidden wisdom behind these urban legends, preparing ourselves to be enlightened, intrigued, and, above all, open to the valuable lessons they offer.

The psychological and cultural significance of urban legends in society.

To understand the significance of urban legends, we must first explore their psychological underpinnings. At their core, urban legends tap into our primal need for storytelling and sense-making. Humans are natural storytellers, seeking to make sense of the world around us and impart wisdom to future generations. Urban legends satisfy this need by offering narratives that explain events and phenomena that elude scientific explanation. Whether it's the tale of a haunted house or a cautionary story about the dangers of meeting strangers online, urban legends provide a framework for understanding the unknown and reaffirming our cultural norms.

The enduring popularity of urban legends can be attributed to their ability to tap into our deepest fears and anxieties. From the fear of the supernatural to the fear of societal collapse, urban legends encapsulate our collective nightmares. They provide a safe space for us to confront and process our fears, allowing us to experience them vicariously through storytelling. This cathartic process ultimately helps us cope with the uncertainties and complexities of modern life. By confronting and discussing these fears, urban legends serve as a form of collective therapy, offering a shared language to navigate the challenges we face.

Furthermore, urban legends are cultural artifacts that bear witness to the values and concerns of a society. Just as ancient myths offer insights into the beliefs and customs of civilizations long gone, urban legends provide a snapshot of our contemporary cultural landscape. For example, the prevalence of urban legends centered around technology and the internet reflects our ever-increasing reliance on these tools. It also speaks to our anxieties surrounding privacy, identity theft, and the potential dangers that lurk in the digital realm. By studying the themes and motifs present in urban legends, researchers can gain valuable insights into the priorities and preoccupations of a particular time and place.

The cultural significance of urban legends is further enhanced by their ability to bridge social divides. These tales are shared and transmitted through our social networks, creating a sense of community and shared experiences. Consider the enthusiasm with which people retell urban legends at social gatherings or during late-night conversations. In this sense, urban legends serve as social glue, connecting individuals through shared narratives and cultural references. They bind us together as a society, fostering a sense of belonging and cohesion amidst a rapidly changing world.

Despite their cultural and psychological significance, urban legends are often dismissed as mere folklore or superstitious beliefs. However, this dismissal overlooks the power and influence these narratives hold over our individual and collective psyches. Urban legends shape our perceptions of morality, influence our decision-making processes, and impact our everyday lives. From cautionary tales about the dangers of interacting with strangers to narratives about miraculous escapes from imminent danger, urban legends inform our behaviors and shape our worldview. They tap into our innate need for storytelling, providing a framework for making sense of the world and exploring our deepest fears and anxieties. As cultural artifacts, urban legends offer insights into the values and concerns of a society, serving as a mirror to our collective psyche.

Their ability to bridge social divides and foster a sense of community contributes to their enduring popularity and influence. As we navigate the complex landscape of a rapidly changing world, urban legends continue to shape and reflect our shared consciousness.

9 798224 455201